IMPERIAL CHINA

Photographs 1850 - 1912

Donald Mennie
*Bridge on the K'un Ming Lake, the Summer
Palace, Peking, 1912-19.*

To Sister Josephine
to remind her of a China
she never saw,
with best wishes

Angelo Tarouta
Christmas 1978

IMPERIAL CHINA

Photographs 1850-1912

Historical texts by Clark Worswick and Jonathan Spence

With a Foreword by Harrison Salisbury

A PENNWICK/CROWN BOOK

ACKNOWLEDGEMENTS

During the course of Clark Worswick's research he traveled to England, Hong Kong and Macao on a grant from the JDR 3rd Fund, which enabled him to select photographs and to do a historical survey of China Coast photography.

The publication accompanies an exhibition jointly organized by the Asia House Gallery of The Asia Society and The American Federation of Arts. Following its premier presentation at the Asia House Gallery in the summer of 1978, the exhibition will travel in the United States under the auspices of The American Federation of Arts.

Appreciation is extended to the following institutions and individuals who made their collections available for the preparation of this book: The Arnold Arboretum of Harvard University, Adam Bartos, The Forbes Library, The Freer Gallery of Art, Martha and Lawrence Friedricks, Sue Hess, R.P. Kingston, Janet and Louis Lehr, Harry Lunn, Jr., The Museum of Modern Art, Richard Pare, The Peabody Museum, Salem, The Royal Asiatic Society, London, The Royal Commonwealth Society, London, Samuel Wagstaff, Jr., Paul Walter, Stuart Cary Welch, Daniel Wolf.

Clark Worswick wishes to acknowledge with gratitude the help and support of Carl Smith who guided research into many 19th century China Coast periodicals concerned with photography. In addition he wishes to thank Jonathan Spence, Allen Wardwell, Wilder Greene, George W. MacDonald, Jr., Peter Chvany, Ray Desmond, John Rosenfield, Bill Jay, Porter McCray, Richard Lanier, and Messrs. Oxam, Lautz and Bush of The China Council of The Asia Society who assisted greatly with oftentimes difficult problems in captioning photographs. Finally, he wishes to thank Marilyn Penn who worked long hours editing a difficult manuscript.

4

Library of Congress Catalogue Card No. 78-55403
ISBN: Clothbound 0-517-533774
ISBN: 0-517-535386, Asia Society Catalogue

Copyright, © Pennwick Publishing, Inc., 1978

Manufactured in the United States of America.

CONTENTS

An unknown poet of the 8th century B.C. wrote of the emperor of China: "Everywhere under the sky is the king's domain — to the farthest ends of the earth all men are his servants." In the 28th year of the People's Republic an interpreter translates a song written in tribute to Chairman Mao Tse-tung as "The working people all over the world have been liberated." When it is gently pointed out that not all workingmen and women have been liberated he concedes error. Ah, yes, he says, the exact phrase is "all men under heaven have been liberated." That is to say, all the Chinese.

China for three or four thousand years has considered itself the center of the world, the center of civilization, the *only* center of civilization. Around China (in the Chinese mind) existed a barbarian world inhabited by races hardly fit to merit the name of human. Whether this belief has really changed in contemporary times is doubtful.

To the Chinese their land has always been the Middle Kingdom. Not a middle kingdom between, say, India and Japan. No, no. The Middle Kingdom between Heaven and Earth, inhabited, true, by humans but humans of a high order, closer to heaven than any other beings.

Appropriately the Mandate of Heaven descends on the ruler of China and when it is withdrawn, as happens from time to time, it is withheld until it again descends on a ruler worthy of the Han people.

The principles so deeply etched upon the minds and morals of China, must be borne in mind if one is to appreciate in full the poignancy and ambiance of the Chinese society celebrated by the remarkable photographs herein assembled. For these mirror a society whose like will never be seen again. Here is the image of a China in dissolution, the Mandate of Heaven stealthily being withdrawn from the last Manchu rulers, penultimately from the extraordinary Dowager Empress who presided over the final extinction of the Middle Kingdom while presuming that her personal mandate was its last best hope.

There never had been such a society in China or anyhwere else — a mixture of ritual, scholarship, ancient rites and art which had its roots in the oldest continual civilization the world has known. Only in recent years, archeologists have uncovered whole villages in the Sian area whose life and artifacts nearly 9,000 years ago differed in no significant way from the life and artifacts of the Chinese village today.

But this 19th century China was in chaos and turmoil—her economics, her industry, her moral standards, her philosophy and way of life being destroyed by the robust and remorseless superior artillery of the European powers. The fiber of China was dissolving in the sweet smoke of opium pipes crammed into Chinese mouths by Western traders. China's coastal cities were being turned into privileged sanctuaries for foreigners who knew not a word of Chinese, nor cared a whit for the analects of Confucius. The incredibly subtle beauty of Chinese art and taste was giving way to the trading demands of clipper skippers.

This produced a confusion of mores and values beyond the power of imagination to conceive. Today, many in China look back upon that time as one of evil and degradation. Europeans perceive in it nostalgia, a *temps perdu,* a dream of *chinoiserie* that covered even the most egregious scabs and running sores.

It is this intermediate moment in history which is captured by the lenses of these photographers, the blend of new and old China, of beauty and misery, of East and West, of Victorian taste and the old Dowager's indulgence, of holiness and horror, luminescent and dungeon-dark, a China that seems now so far back in history that one wonders if, indeed, it ever had an existence.

Harrison Salisbury

7

IMPERIAL CHINA: A CHINESE VIEW
by Jonathan Spence

The Chinese government in 1860 was, paradoxically, both weak and powerful. It is not surprising that the Westerners who began to visit China at this time, and to photograph it, were puzzled by what they found. Contemporary Chinese officials and intellectuals were similarly anxious and uncertain.

The weakness was evidenced most spectacularly by internal civil war, by financial crisis, and by vulnerability to the pressures of foreign imperialism. The Taiping Rebellion, which raged in China from 1851 to 1864, was only one of four major risings which plagued the rulers at this time, and which occurred in every corner of the empire — from Yunnan in the southwest to Kansu in the northwest, from Shantung in the northeast down to the environs of Canton in the southeast. The ruling Manchus — government at this time being in the hands of the Empress Dowager Tz'u-hsi who ruled as regent for her infant son T'ung-chih — were unable either to finance the suppression campaigns or to provide adequate troops in the regular armies. They were forced to rely on regionally recruited Chinese armies, funded by provincial revenues or new sources of commercial taxation, backed by networks of local militia controlled by the rural gentry. Nor could the Manchus, in such a plight, withstand the foreigners effectively; the burning of the Summer Palace near Peking, in the summer of 1860, was but the most spectacular offshoot of a foreign policy of procrastination and bombast that had been followed since before the Opium War of 1839.

Yet, at the same time, there were some obvious strengths: China did not fall apart, and the Manchus kept their throne. The rebellions were slowly and painfully suppressed; the financial system (much aided, it is true, by the inauguration of the Imperial Maritime Customs Service under Western management) was restored to viability; and the foreigners were won over to a calmer frame of mind by a new round of treaties that gave increased commercial and evangelical opportunities, as well as a definitively low tax on the imports of opium from India. Senior officials of the Chinese Empire launched a program of moral Confucian regeneration, designed to retrieve the ethical ground lost in the long years of rebellion, and officals both in the provinces and in Peking began to study aspects of Western military technology and international law, and to train a small number of subordinates in foreign languages. A small number of Chinese students were even sent to study in the United States (page 70).

But though the Ch'ing dynasty was to last another fifty years — the last emperor abdicated in 1912 — China had suffered a terrible series of blows, and the Manchus could not carry through the kind of reform program that the nation needed for successful survival. It is this hindsight that gives the early photographs we see here such precise poignance, for the Chinese faces and landscapes that we gaze at are giving us contradictory messages: the people and the land have always been like this, they say, and yet we know that the mere fact of their being photographed portends that things will never be viewed like this again.

It was only after the Treaty Settlements of 1860 that Westerners were, for the first time, allowed to travel with some freedom around China. Not surprisingly, the initial photographs are often of Chinese in Hong Kong or the treaty ports — those ports such as Shanghai, Canton and Ningpo opened to foreign residence and trade by the Western victories in war. The Chinese posing here, from whichever walk of life, confront a lens made possible only by act of war; and the Westerners strolling Chinese streets did so as conquerors, however unwittingly, not as tourists or explorers in a general sense. There is no need to think of these treaty port Chinese as all changed, however, though it is true that they were now free to change in new ways; it was only slowly that a group of Chinese with views that had not been possible before did emerge in the last thirty years of the nineteenth century. These were the men of the "littoral" who absorbed elements of Western science, political theory and journalistic techniques along with their visual stimuli of roof, ship and steeple.

Few men in the China of this time capture the overlays of traditionalism and change more movingly than the junior official Wu K'o-tu. Wu came from a literati family in Kansu province, in China's northwest, an area that had been struck by a major rebellion of the local Moslem population in the late 1860s but was still, of course, far from the areas of Western penetration. He had risen through the ranks of the bureaucracy to become a censor, and had gained some reputation for his outspokenness on controversial issues. On the vexed question of whether foreign envoys should have to kowtow before the emperor, for example, Wu had argued in the negative. Since the foreigners had no knowledge of correct ethical behavior, he argued, and sought only material profit from their actions, there was no point in requesting them to follow ritual observances based on Confucian moral premises; to do so would make no more sense than assembling a group of sheep and pigs and having them dance to music. Wu was later demoted from office, but after a period of retirement in his home in Kansu he returned to Peking to take up office once again, this time with the more junior rank of Secretary in the Board of Civil Office. He was deeply distressed by the way that the Empress Dowager manipulated the succession after the death of her son, T'ung-chih, in 1875. By choosing a new heir from T'ung-chih's own generation, the Empress Dowager kept her own power as regent, but went against all the laws of generational succession laid down during the Ch'ing and previous dynasties. Wu protested her act as a Chinese traditionalist, not as a Manchu sympathizer; since his junior rank precluded his addressing the Empress Dowager directly, he killed himself to give weight to his protest. As he told the Empress Dowager in a message he drafted to her before his death, his protest grew both from his sense of devotion to his rulers and out of fear for the West and the changes it might bring: "Promote peace and prosperity," he wrote, "by appointing only worthy men to public office; do not strive after those things that the foreigners hold so dear, thus will our country be preserved; do not initiate actions that our founding rulers refused to initiate, thus will our descendants still have happiness."[1] And in the same vigorous and clear classical language, writing to his own son a few hours later and explaining his decision to kill himself, Wu directed that he should be buried close to the tomb of the late Emperor T'ung-chih, not in the family burial ground in Kansu. Propriety would not be offended, Wu felt, since his brother had predeceased him and lay already beside the graves of their parents. "No doubt you will desire to take home my remains," Wu admonished, "but do not do so. What you may do is take the small photograph that I had made when I left Peking and have a full portrait made from it in our home, and bring that together with my robes to the family cemetery."[2] The photograph was not yet of high enough status for burial as proxy for the living body, but its accuracy — Wu used the phrase *chao-hsiang,* "likeness made via reflected light" — was unquestioned.

So we see that Wu could warn his rulers against foreign innovations whilst using them himself, and one can be sure he was not aware of paradox. But in the 1880s and 1890s, an increasingly virulent anti-foreignism grew among the Chinese gentry just as foreign technology was increasingly adopted by certain senior provincial officials.[3] This anti-foreignism sprang from many roots: from the memory of military defeat in two wars, which became three after the French victories in the wars of 1884, and four after the shattering victories of the Japanese in 1894-95; from the soaring sales of foreign opium and other dislocations caused by foreign trade; from Christian missionary behavior in the interior of China, particularly in remote rural areas, and from fear of the Chinese converts as presenting a new kind of threat to China from within. Antagonism was expressed in a gamut of ways that ranged from rumor, scurrilous literature, obscene drawings and placards, down to physical harassment and riots that led to injury or death.

At the same time, the prestige of foreign technology began to enter ever more deeply into the fabric of Chinese society, and with it an awareness of the tenets of social Darwinism that seemed to do so much to explain the reasons behind the startling material power of the West, and to add urgency to China's own search for "self-strengthening" if she were to avoid an evolutionary death. Foreign schools, not only in the treaty ports, but elsewhere in China, began to teach scientific and mechanical engineering skills; powerful Chinese governors-general made arms in modern arsenals, advised by foreign staffs; they even assembled (and partly constructed) steamships that could compete successfully with foreign lines; developed mines and industrial plants; and, having first rejected railways as harmful, began now to seek Chinese economic control over the new lengths of track that Western consortia had demanded the rights to lay.

The depth of feeling with which Western technology could be absorbed is dramatically shown in the case of K'ang Yu-wei. K'ang, a brilliant classical scholar from southeast China, had, like Wu K'o-tu, prepared for a civil service career by taking the traditional examinations; but he had also read as widely as he could in translations of Western scientific and political works. By the mid-1880s, as China was defeated by the French (the third of her disastrous wars with foreign powers), K'ang began to sketch in outline the book for which he is now best known, the *Ta-t'ung shu* or "Study of the Great Unity."

In K'ang's eclectic and visionary book, Confucian, Buddhist and Scientistic elements blended with Western missionary elements into a utopian formulation. K'ang wrote of a time in which national tensions would be abolished along with national boundaries, when the new industrial skills would be harmonized with pooled natural resources in the interests of a raised world standard of living, when the differentiations between the sexes would fade as each gender was reared, educated, trained and dressed alike. In an era of perfected machinery man would be freed from the drudgeries of labor and able to devote himself to culture and the arts, as his health was watched over by a skillful and benevolent corps of medical experts. Swift motion would enrich all lives, and the elements be overcome as transport and communications systems were perfected: "In the beginning of the period of Great Unity people will live on the mountain tops; in the middle period they will live on the sea; in the final period they will live in the air," K'ang wrote.

K'ang leaped, with such speculations, far above the mundane problems that faced Ch'ing China in its declining years — though in his daily life he was an activist who was concerned with practical political affairs at both the provincial and the national level, and sought to reinterpret Confucianism by tracing reformist elements in the earliest formulations of Confucius' teachings. After years of working through study societies and journalistic writings to make his views known, K'ang was summoned (in January 1898) to present his views to the Tsungli Yamen, the Peking bureau specializing in foreign affairs. And though (or perhaps because) officials at that meeting declared K'ang to be "high-flown" and "crazy," the young emperor, who was in despair at China's ever-weakening international position, summoned K'ang to write to him directly, and in June 1898, the two men finally met when K'ang was summoned to audience at the court. His statement of his premise was forceful: "The prerequisites of reform are that all the laws and the political and social systems be changed and decided anew, before it can be called a reform. Now those who talk about reform only change some specific affairs, and do not reform the institutions."[4] Relying on the traditionally-oriented and conservative Chinese officials to carry through reforms of such a nature would, argued K'ang, be "like climbing a tree to seek for fish."

Partly inspired by such sentiments, and also chafing increasingly under the continued supervision of the Empress Dowager, the emperor launched an ambitious program of reform in the summer of 1898, summoning K'ang Yu-wei as one of his advisers. But the speed and comprehensiveness of the projected reforms were too much for most senior officials, and in a reactionary counter-coup the Empress Dowager returned to power, the emperor was put under "palace arrest," and K'ang Yu-wei was exiled. Thus it was, ironically, in the hill town of Darjeeling — the prototypical summer retreat for the wives of the rulers of British India — that K'ang Yu-wei revised the earlier drafts of his original *Ta-T'ung shu* for publication, which he completed in 1902.

K'ang's influence and originality were great. As one scholar wrote recently, he was "determined to confront the implications of a larger world with a diversity of civilizations" and to show that "China's old hierarchies were simply parochial."[5] But by the early 1900s, K'ang was already appearing conservative to a new generation of radical Chinese. These men, joined now by a growing number of emancipated Chinese women who had been educated in the new schools, looked beyond the imperial Chinese tradition altogether, to a world in which China would seize the most potent of all Western secrets — that of republican constitutional government. To achieve this end they were willing to defy the state in small revolutionary societies, and to employ the means of insurrection and assassination.

These Chinese of the early twentieth century lived with a heightened sense of crisis in a country that, they felt, might very soon cease to exist as an independent entity. The disastrous French war of 1884 had been followed by the even more shattering defeat at the hands of the Japanese in 1894. In the peace treaty that followed, China had to cede Taiwan to Japan, and was only saved from having to cede much of Manchuria as well by the prolonged opposition of the Western powers who were uneasy at Japan's growing strength. In 1898, the Germans seized Tsingtao in Shantung, and consolidated their hold of the territory around the city; British, French and Russians all responded by forming their own tighter "spheres of influence." The Boxer Rising of 1900, with its anti-foreign, anti-Christian and anti-technological aspects, led to fresh humiliations for China as the allied forces occupied Peking and collected a vast indemnity.

The fear and anger of these days were well caught in pamphlets like Ch'en T'ien-hua's "Clarion Bell for the Age" where the intuitive sense of the Boxers was given express form: foreign imperialism, if allowed to continue unchecked, meant genocide for the Chinese. "Ayah, ayah! They're coming, they're coming! What are coming? The foreigners! The foreigners are coming! It's no good for anybody: old, young, men, women, high, low, rich, poor, officials, scholars, merchants, craftsmen, all types of people from now on will be the sheep and cattle in the foreigners' corral, the fish and meat in their pots. They will be able to kill us if they wish, boil us if they want."[6] For other students, though foreign imperialism was a major danger, the Manchus themselves were the target of priority, for it was their weakness and ineptitude that was keeping down the Han Chinese people and preventing them from seizing the opportunity that history offered. Such views received their most coherent first expression from the pen of Tsou Jung, in his savage pamphlet *The Revolutionary Army*, published in 1903. Tsou, born in western China (in Szechwan) in 1885, had rebelled against his examination-centered classical education, and had gone instead to Japan for his studies. There he had read quite widely in Western history and political theory and gained a centralizing vision that pitted Western constitutional strengths and Darwinian drives against the weak and increasingly ineffective Manchu state. For Tsou, the Han Chinese must rediscover their racial identities, repel the Manchus and so gain the strength from the West to repel the West in their turn. He used the image both of the microscope and the photograph to express the scrutiny to which he wished to subject his own people and his polity, a scrutiny that led him to this conclusion:

> "When the thirteen states [of America] became independent, the German states formed a confederacy, and Italy united itself, as we read in their revolutionary histories, public opinion was roused to such a degree that war was declared on the monarchy, the mother country overthrown, and the aristocracy killed off. They spoke out for freedom and forcefully upheld self-rule. Internally they prepared themselves for war, externally they resisted powerful neighbors. During a time of military ravages, when the whole country was being devastated, they never stopped making great plans. From parliament and constitution down to local government, they kept everyday administration running, and set the highest standards for mankind."[7]

Tsou called for the necessary Chinese Washingtons and Napoleons to rise up and seize the freedoms they required; he called on China to proudly accept the "Yellow Peril" epithet the West had bestowed upon them, and ended with a triumphant challenge to his countrymen: "You possess government, run it yourselves; you have laws, guard them yourselves; you have industries, administer them yourselves; you possess armed forces, order them yourselves; you possess lands, watch over them yourselves; you have inexhaustible resources, exploit them yourselves."[8]

Tsou Jung was jailed for these words, and he died in prison in 1906. But his death came from natural causes, and it is ironic that his tract was only published at all initially because of the protection offered by the foreign settlement in Shanghai. The Western enclaves gave shelter from Manchu reprisals to many such Chinese nationalists, and few Westerners could see that beyond the newly-strident anti-Manchu nationalism lay an anti-Western nationalism that would run just as deep.

In these dying days of the dynasty, Westerners traveled widely within and across China. The best of them carried out their observations with a mixture of acuteness and affection, whatever their overt reasons for travel were: some were seeking mineral resources, some searching for new flora, others surveying potential railway tracks or seeking new areas of evangelism. The camera became an increasingly intimate part of this reconnaissance, and if it was directed often at the grotesque and the distorted so it caught, too, the beautiful, the fleeting moment. China's immensity swallowed up its visitors, as it does again today. Few knew much of the politics of the time, or had much sense of the tensions and angers that lay behind Chinese deference or courtesy. The Manchu dynasty seemed, in its very last years, to be finally adapting to a world of Western values on Western terms. The classical examination system was abolished in 1905; delegations were sent to study Western governmental practices; a program of constitutional development was announced that brought provincial assemblies into being in 1909, and a national assembly in Peking a year later; the army was equipped and reorganized along Western lines; the old Grand Council was replaced by a modern-looking cabinet. But the Chinese students, working in Japan or the United States or Europe and returning home, were either unimpressed by these changes or else stimulated by them to ask for more. In seeing eternal verities in a Chinese face or a Chinese landscape, the Western observers lost their chance to catch the mood of restlessness that lay beneath.

There is nothing surprising in this. The changes taking place within China were vast but also episodic, widely scattered geographically, uncoordinated, undirected. Few leaders credited with spearheading nationalist revolutions can have had less contact with the ramifications of their own movements than Sun Yat-sen between 1906 and 1911. Yet it was Sun Yat-sen's revolutionary T'ung-meng hui party that played a key part in leading the insurrections in 1911 that cost the Manchus their throne, and led to the enforced abdication of the last emperor — the boy P'u-yi — in February, 1912. In the chaos of the warlord years that followed, China was thrown open ever more widely to Western economic penetration and to the force of Western political ideas. With the Manchus gone, surprisingly easily, the Chinese were to discover how difficult the underlying problems in their society truly were.

If any one Westerner can be called upon to summon up the anticipation of an unknown future from the basis of his own Ch'ing past, it should perhaps be Sir Robert Hart, the Belfast-born distiller's son, who arrived in China in 1854 and ran the Chinese Imperial Maritime Customs from 1861 until his retirement in 1908, and died in 1911 only a few days before the dynasty fell. Near the end of his life, Hart pointed to two important areas that the West seemed to him to have stupidly neglected. First, a central factor in the West's assault on China had been the desire for cornering markets in the hope of vast future gain; but, as Hart pointed out, "the paying or buying [Chinese] public exists more in fanciful estimates than in sober reality, — and so I think all these schemes will be ruinous in the end." Second, something profoundly important lay behind the Boxer uprisings of 1900, something far beyond primitive xenophobia, frustrated patriotism or anti-Christianity. "In fifty years' time," guessed Hart, "there will be millions of Boxers in serried ranks and war's panoply at the call of the Chinese Government: there is not the slightest doubt of that." Such men, Hart felt, "armed, drilled, disciplined, and animated by patriotic — if mistaken — motives, will make residence in China impossible for foreigners, will take back from foreigners everything foreigners have taken from China." It was a surprising forecast from the man who had also summed up his life's work as being this: "We have helped to keep China quiet and the dynasty on its legs, and I hope this is something."[9] Perhaps the answer to the apparent paradox is that Hart, like many of the photographers in China at this time, was seeing more than he knew.

Footnotes

1. Wu K'o-tu: his farewell memorials are translated in Evan Morgan, *A Guide to Wenli Styles and Chinese Ideals* (Shanghai, 1912), pp. 258-78. Wu's biography is given in Arthur Hummel, ed., *Eminent Chinese of the Ch'ing Period* (Washington, D.C., 1944), pp. 874-75. A fine analysis of this general period is given in Mary C. Wright, *The Last Stand of Chinese Conservatism, the T'ung-chih Restoration, 1862-1874* (Stanford University Press, 1957).

2. Evan Morgan, *A Guide to Wenli Styles and Chinese Ideals* (Shanghai, 1912), pp. 258-78.

3. For an analysis of Chinese anti-missionary activities see Paul Cohen, *China and Christianity: the Missionary Movement and the Growth of Chinese Antiforeignism, 1860-1870* (Harvard University Press, 1963); and for the men of the "littoral" see the same author's *Between Tradition and Modernity: Wang T'ao and Reform in Late Ch'ing China* (Harvard University Press, 1974).

4. K'ang Yu-wei's *Ta-t'ung shu* has been translated by Laurence G. Thompson, *Ta T'ung Shu: The One World Philosophy of K'ang Yu-wei* (London, 1958). His autobiography and related studies are printed in *K'ang Yu-wei, A Biography and a Symposium*, ed. Lo Jung-pang (University of Arizona Press, 1967). The quotation on reform is taken from Immanuel Hsu, *The Rise of Modern China* (Oxford University Press, 1976), p. 452.

5. Don C. Price, *Russia and the Roots of the Chinese Revolution, 1896-1911* (Harvard University Press, 1974), p. 16.

6. Ch'en T'ien-hua's "Clarion Bell" is cited in Joseph Esherick, *Reform and Revolution in China: The 1911 Revolution in Hunan and Hubei* (University of California Press, 1976).

7. Tsou Jung's *The Revolutionary Army*, translated by John Lust (The Hague, 1968), p. 100.

8. Ibid., p. 126.

9. The quotations from Robert Hart's *These From the Land of Sinim* are discussed in Jonathan Spence, *To Change China: Western Advisers in China 1620-1960* (Boston, 1969), pp. 124-28.

PHOTOGRAPHS

M. Miller
A Canton Lady, 1861-64.

Photography in China began in 1846
when Hugh Mackay opened the first
daguerrotype establishment in far-Asia.
By 1870 there had emerged three
geniuses of the China photographic
scene: Beato, Thomson, and Miller.
Miller's specialty was the Chinese sitter
whom he photographed with great
understanding. In this studio portrait he
used to advantage the standard
photographic conventions of the China
Coast — the full-face portrait, the
costumed figure and the ubiquitous vase
and flower.

CANTON.

No. 201, GENERAL VIEW—WOOCHOW CITY.

On the left of our View, the large building in course of erection is a Chinese Theatre, the other buildings are Chinese Hongs, forming the back ground are the Woochow Hills—in front is the West River, covered with Chinese Sampans—these boats are the only places of abode of many Chinese and their families.

Photographer Unknown
Panorama of Wu-chou, Kwangsi, 1870s.

Wu-chou was the gateway to Kwangsi
Province. Two hundred miles
up-river from Macao, it was made a
treaty port in 1897.

John Thomson
*I-hsin, the First Prince Kung (1833-98),
Peking, 1871-72.*

Upon the death of the Hsien-feng
Emperor (1861), Prince Kung, the
brother of the late emperor, was raised to
the position of Prince Adviser to the
throne. Prince Kung acted as a
stabilizing element in Chinese politics
and as an important negotiator with the
foreigners from 1860 until the 1880s.

Opposite

Yu, Court Photographer
*The Empress Dowager, Tz'u-hsi, and the
Imperial Eunuchs, Peking, 1902-08.*

Tz'u-hsi was the real power behind the
Chinese throne. One of the most
extraordinary women of the 19th
century, she had great ambition and
remarkable political expertise. After
backing the ill-fated Boxer Uprising in
1900, she softened her lifelong hostility
to foreigners.
  Front right is Li Lien-ying, her chief
palace eunuch.

Photographer Unknown
The Forbidden City from Coal Hill, 1901.

Within Peking was the Imperial City and within the Imperial City was the Purple Forbidden City, the actual dwelling place of the emperors, with its roofs covered with yellow tile. The Forbidden City, built by the Ming dynasty in the 15th century, contained houses, temples, theatres, audience halls and libraries.

Yu, Court Photographer
The Empress Dowager and Royal Group in a Palace Courtyard, Peking, 1902-08.

Photographer Unknown
A Section of the Great Wall, 1901.

Begun in the 3rd century B.C. the Great
Wall stretched from the Gulf of Chihli
1500 miles westward to the gates of
central Asia. It remains the largest single
structure ever built by man.

E.H. Wilson
Au-lan Suspension Bridge,
Western Szechwan, June 16, 1908.

This three-hundred yard bamboo bridge
crosses the Ta-tu River, a tributary of the
Yangtze River in Szechwan Province at
Kuan-hsien.

26

M. Miller
A Shanghai Lady, 1861-64.

M. Miller
*Liu Ch'ang-yu, The Governor-General
of Kwangtung and Kwangsi, Canton,
1862-63.*

The son of a Hunanese merchant, Liu
was active in the bloody suppression of
the Taiping Rebellion. During 1863-67,
he was the governor of Chihli, one of
the most powerful positions in China.

M. Miller
Scene by the Road, Hong Kong, 1861-64.

28

M. Miller
Cantonese Mandarin and His Wife,
1861-64.

Entrance to the nine grades of the
Mandarinate was by competitive
examination. In addition to silk animal
squares worn on the chest of an official,
hatspikes, jewels and peacock feathers
and formal belt fittings denoted the rank
of the wearer.

M. Miller
Queen's Road, Hong Kong, 1861-64.

Ceded to the British by the Viceroy at
Canton (January, 1841), Hong Kong
quickly became the favored base for
smuggling illicit Indian opium into
China. In the 1840s it took six months
for a letter to reach Europe, and a year
to complete a simple commercial
transaction with London. But by the late
1850s, Hong Kong boasted almost two
miles of roads, and it had become the
staging area for the European Opening of
China by force of arms.

Opposite

Attributed to Weed & Howard
The Executive Council, Hong Kong, 1860.

Sir Hercules Robinson (with top hat),
Governor; Col. Haythorne, Chief of
Staff in China; Mercer (left), the
Colonial Secretary; and Mr. Leslie
(standing).

The Decline of Imperial China

The period 1840-60 marked the bloody culmination of the imperial court's failure to deal with serious domestic and foreign problems. Within China's borders, increasing dissatisfaction with repressive government measures had swelled the ranks of countless secret societies which the neglected military was hard put to eliminate. On China's southern shore, foreign merchants pressured the court for changes in the system of foreign trade at the same time that their trade in opium was disturbing China's balance of payments. A hard-line group of officials won the policy debate but only brought on the First Opium War (1839-42) by their actions. In defeat, the court, now under the influence of conciliation-minded officials, conceded the right to set customs duties, the right of extraterritoriality, and the opening of five treaty ports along the southeast coast.

Partly because of the deepening economic crisis and partly because of the new phase of foreign penetration, there erupted a series of massive popular revolts. The first was the Taiping Rebellion, which began in 1850 and spread to the Yangtze valley in 1853. The imperial forces were only able to extirpate the Taipings in 1864. Simultaneously, they had to deal with rebellion by the Nien (1853-68) and the Moslems (1853-78). The court also faced new foreign pressure for greater access to China, and again responded with a hard line. The result was the Second Opium War, another defeat, more concessions, and the disgrace of the Anglo-French capture of Canton, Tientsin, and Peking, and the Russian annexation of large tracts of land in the northwest.

32

Felix Beato
Taku Forts After the Allied Attack,
August 21, 1860.

Commanding the riverine approaches to Peking were the Taku Forts. The linchpin of the defense of North China, the forts were thought to be impregnable. But, on August 21, 1860, a combined Anglo-French force attacked and stormed the forts. Accompanying the army was Felix Beato, who fortuitously made the following series of photographs of China's Opening to the West.

Overleaf

Felix Beato
Panorama of the Abandoned Fort, Pei-t'ang
August, 1860.

At the time this photograph was taken, Prince Seng had 30,000 Chinese cavalry — 6,000 of whom were Mongols — poised to attack the Anglo-French Expeditionary Force. Instead, he chose to delay his attack. In mid-September, Prince Seng's army was defeated; Prince Seng was later reduced in rank, and forced to serve in the army as a private soldier.

Felix Beato
Interior of One of the Taku Forts
After Explosion of the Magazine,
August 21, 1860.

Garnet Wolsely, an eyewitness to the explosion, described it as a "tall black pillar, bursting like a rocket after it had attained great height, (then) a vast shower of wood and earth." Inside the fort he found, "the magazine lay in heaps everywhere, intermingled with overturned cannon, broken gun carriages, and the dead and wounded."

38

Felix Beato
*Lake with the Summer Palace Beyond,
Peking,* October, 1860.

The Summer Palace contained over two-
hundred buildings, thirty of which were
imperial palaces designed with the
assistance of Jesuit architects.

Felix Beato
Prince Kung After Formally Offering the Ch'ing Dynasty's Surrender to the Allies, Peking, November 4, 1860.

Opposite

Felix Beato
The Yuan Ming Yuan (The Old Summer Palace), 1860.

The death of hostages seized under a flag of truce, and Chinese reluctance to honor treaty obligations caused Lord Elgin to order the burning of the Summer Palace complex on October 18, 1860. Before it was put to the torch, Beato made the only known photographs of the palaces.

43

44

Foreign Expansion in China

Upon the Opening of China to the West, the European visitor discovered a country vastly different from his expectations. Despite its huge resource of manpower, China was a land with inadequate roads and with an extensive lock and canal system that had fallen into grave disrepair. This first impression of technological backwardness and economic ruin led the world powers to conceive of China as an easy mark for territorial and economic expansion, as well as a substantial trade market with its 300 million customers. Telegraphs were constructed, mines opened, cotton mills built. When it was discovered in 1895 that China had only 195 miles of railways, Belgian, French, Russian, British, and American banks all competed for the right to grant the construction loan for the 768 mile Peking-Hankow line, the first railway that would link the imperial capital to the heartland of China.

Photographer Unknown
Railway Right-of-way Alongside the City Walls, Peking, 1899-1905.

Tracks leading to the terminus of the Peking-Hankow line at the Ch'ien-men Gate.

46

M. Miller
Cotton Broker, Canton, 1861-64.

Donald Mennie
Stupa at the Jade Cloud Temple, the
Western Hills, Peking, 1912-19.

The temple complex of which this was a
part was founded during the Yuan
dynasty (13th century), but this stupa
was constructed in 1748 by the Ch'ien-
lung Emperor, who also built a small
palace nearby.

48

Donald Mennie
Through the Nan Hsi Men, Peking,
1912-19.

This gateway is the most western of the
three gates in the south wall of the city.

Opposite

John Thomson
The Wu-shan Gorge, Szechwan, 1868-72.

50

M. Miller
Shopkeepers at Canton, 1861-64.

M. Miller
Mandarin and Son, Canton, 1861-64.

52

John Thomson
*A Pagoda in South China, Near
Ch'ao-chou fu, 1868-72.*

53

E.H. Wilson
Northwest of I-ch'ang, Terraced Fields,
Farmhouse and Limestone Cliffs, 1910.

54

John Thomson
Figure Posed on Steps with
Village Beyond, 1868-72.

Attributed to Dr. John McCosh
The Chen-hai-lou, The Five-Story Pagoda, Canton, 1851.

A salted paper print from a calotype negative, this is the earliest surviving photograph of imperial China. McCosh is known to have had equipment capable of producing a picture of this size and in 1851, while on a two year sick-leave from the Bengal Army to visit the Cape of Good Hope, New South Wales and China, he presumably made this picture.

John Thomson
House of the Official, Yang, Peking,
1871-72.

**Emil Rusfeldt, The Hong Kong
Photographic Company**
*Interior, the Temple of the Five-Hundred
Genjii in Canton, 1871-74.*

58

Attributed to W. Saunders
Fukien Temple, Ningpo, Chekiang Province,
1870-75.

Donald Mennie
The Mid-day Meal, Peking, 1912-19.

A restaurant where coolies or caravan attendants could eat steaming bowls of congee, noodles, and tea. The advertisement in the background is for the "Benevolent Pill".

61

John Thomson
Abbot and Monks of the Kushan Monastery,
1868-72.

Photographer Unknown
Three Women in the Cangue, Shanghai,
1907.

Notes on Chinese Punishment

The penal system in imperial China was direct and uncompromising. Every member of a family was responsible for each other, while the father was liable for the misdeeds of all. In turn, the head of each district was held personally responsible for misdemeanors of any member of his district; this chain of responsibility went on in endless gradations to the highest officers of government. Any trial was an ordeal by punishment until the accused confessed, and then the penalty was swift and specific:

HOUSEBREAKING AND THEFT
The Cangue.
The person was compelled to stand in front of the house or store which he had violated for a specified time during which all of his functions had to be performed while imprisoned in this restraining device.

HIGHWAY ROBBERY
Crucifixion or Decapitation.

GRAVE ROBBERY
Carrying the Crate.
The criminal was placed in a wooden crate from which his head protruded and left to die of starvation or heatstroke.

BRIGANDAGE
Standing in the Tub.
The person was placed in a vat-like tub filled with unslaked lime with a hole at the top for his head. Each day some of the bricks that he stood on were removed until eventually, the accused was eaten by the lime.

TREASON
The Death of a Thousand Cuts.
The culprit was whittled away a joint at a time until his body was cut into pieces by the executioner.

62

Attributed to W. Saunders
Execution Scene, Shanghai, 1870s.

64

Photographer Unknown
Group of Criminals Condemned to
Execution, Canton, 1890s

Photographer Unknown
The Execution Ground, Canton, 1870s

Attributed to M. Rossier or Felix Beato
*Viceroy Yeh Ming-ch'en, Viceroy of Canton,
Canton, 1858, (Rossier), or Calcutta, 1859,
(Beato).*

The son of a village apothecary, Yeh had
risen to the position of Governor-
General of Kwantung and Kwangsi.
Exceptionally brutal, he boasted of
having put to death more than 100,000
rebels, 70,000 of them in a six-month
period during 1855. In 1858, he was
captured by the British during the
Second Opium War and exiled to
Calcutta, where he died a year later.

Opposite

John Thomson
Nanking Arsenal, 1868-72.

Outside the city, near the site of the
Porcelain Tower, this was one of the first
modern arsenals in China.

John Thomson
Manchu Bannermen, Canton, 1868-72.

The troops of the eight Manchu Banners (headed by great princes of the royal family) were instrumental in conquering China and creating the Ch'ing dynasty in the 17th century. As the bulwark of the army, the Banners were settled around Peking and were discouraged from intermarrying with the Chinese.

Opposite

M. Miller
Hong Kong Parade Ground, May 24, 1862.

Opposite

Photographer Unknown
Chinese School Boys Sent to America, Hong Kong, 1872.

Between 1872 and 1875, 120 Chinese boys from poor families in South China were sent to the United States to be educated. Settled in towns and villages in the Connecticut Valley, they learned English as well as singing, dancing and piano playing.

M. Miller
Yeng Chong, Compradore, Smith, Kennedy & Co., Hankow, 1861-64.

The entire China trade rested on an elaborate symbiosis of European and Chinese merchants who provided each other with reciprocal markets. Compradores, like Yeng Chong, became enormously wealthy as middle-men and as managers of European firms in China.

71

72

Photographer Unknown
Stationery Street, Canton, 1870s.

M. Miller
Chinese Translators, Canton, 1861-64.

74

M. Miller
Compradores, Canton, 1861-64.

Attributed to Weed & Howard or M. Miller
Pedders Wharf, Hong Kong, 1860-61.

Emil Rusfeldt
The Hong Kong Photographic Rooms,
Opposite The Germanic Club, at Wellington
and Wyndham Streets, 1871-74.

Photography in China

Inaccessible to most Westerners for centuries before the Opium Wars (1839-1860), imperial China was a particularly fertile environment for photography when it arrived on the China coast. Where previous generations could rely only on fanciful tales and legends of the last great hidden empire, the camera provided 19th century Europe and America with the means to separate myth from fact. Despite arduous and primitive working conditions and initial suspicion of the camera as an "evil eye," photography succeeded in preserving the last moments of a millennia-old culture poised on the brink of change.

The documentation of China by both European and Chinese photographers was extraordinarily comprehensive. It included the massive landscapes of the Yangtze Gorges, the mountains of the western Szechwan provinces and the jungles which had long been used as places of banishment for those exiled by the imperial court. Additionally, architectural landmarks such as the Great Wall, the imperial Summer Palace complex, and Peking with its graceful pagodas, temples and streets were all unending subjects of interest for the photographer's eye. Through the portraits of different classes of people at work, at leisure, in the street, and in the studio, photography affords us a detailed inside view of the diversity and splendor of one of the world's oldest living cultures.

artist copying a Photograph

Photographer Unknown
Chinese Artist Copying Photograph for the Export Trade, Hong Kong, 1860s.

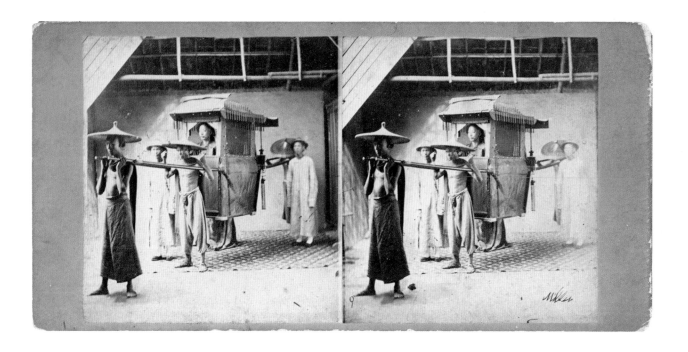

These illustration show the three types of
photographs available through a China
Coast studio in the early 1860s: the *carte
de visite*, the stereographic view and the
full plate print.

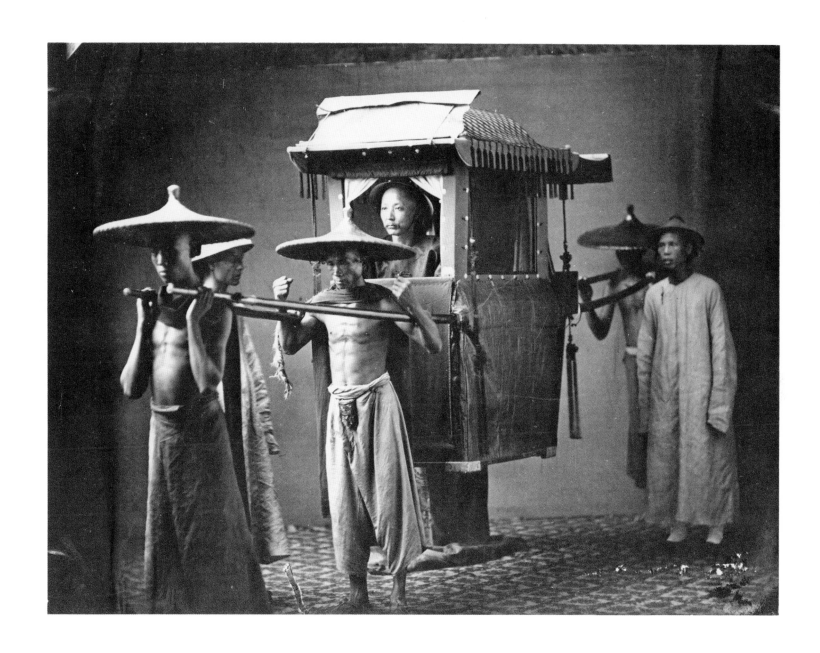

M. Miller
Official at Canton on a Visit, Three states,
1861-64.

80

14334. Chinese Dentistry, Canton, China.

Photographer Unknown
Chinese Dentistry, Canton, 1900.

Stereoscopic view for mass Western
consumption.

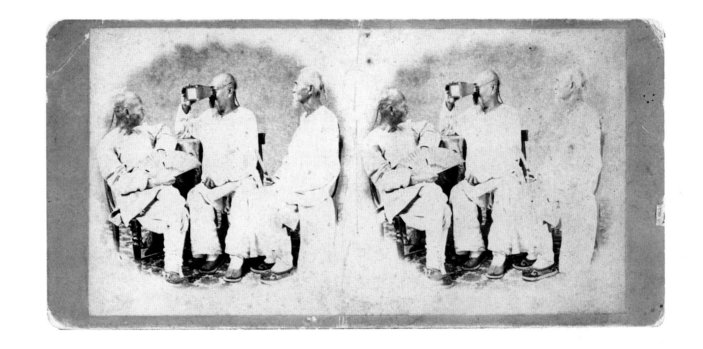

M. Miller
Three Chinese with Viewer, Canton,
1861-64.

A rare view of Chinese people posed
with photographic apparatus. The
photograph itself has been taken with
Miller's characteristic sympathy for his
subjects.

Two stereographic views that demonstrate the hardening of Western imperialist attitudes in China during the 19th century, and show the changing way China was presented in the West during the period 1860-1900.

82

The American Consul's Four-in-Hand, Hong Kong, China
Copyright 1896 by Strohmeyer & Wyman.

M. Miller
English Merchants and Chinese Translators on Picnic, Canton, 1861-64.

Photographer Unknown
The American Consul's Four-in-Hand, Hong Kong, 1890s

John Thomson
Chinese Types, 1868-72.

M. Rossier
French Troops, Canton, 1858.

Part of the stereo series released by
Negretti & Zambra in 1859 that detailed
the sights and scenes of Canton after it
was captured by the 5,679 man allied
Anglo-French Expeditionary Force.

34. Officers of the Japanese army at Peking. China.
Copyright 1902 by C. H. Graves.

Photographer Unknown
Japanese Officers, Peking, 1900.

In 1900, traditionalist, anti-foreign
Boxers joined imperial troops to besiege
the foreign legations at Peking. For fifty-
five days the siege continued until a
multinational relief force fought its way
up from Tientsin and rescued the
inhabitants of the legations.

86

Photographer Unknown
Opium Den, Canton, 1900.

A stereoscopic view for the Western
market.

Watching the "Foreign Devils"—Gate of the English Bridge barring the Cantonese from the Legations, China. Copyright 1900 by Underwood & Underwood.

Photographer Unknown
Watching the Foreign Devils. The Gateway of the English Bridge Barring Chinese from the Western Legations, Canton, 1900.

During the late imperial period, forty-eight treaty ports were opened to European trade and residence. Within the treaty ports, the foreigners established their own European-style residential compounds and official buildings.

M. MILLER
Hong Kong, 1861-64

During the 19th century, no photographer of the Chinese scene revealed as much empathy for the Chinese sitter as Miller. Taken more than 115 years ago, his photographs have a penetrating psychological quality that is distinctly modern.

88

89

Miller Photograph # 10. A Mandarin and His Family, Canton, 1861-64.

90

M. Miller
Wife of a Mandarin, Canton, 1861-64.

M. Miller
A Pregnant Girl in Macao, 1861-64.

92

M. Miller
Douglas Lapraik, Merchant, Hong Kong,
1861-64.

One of the leading British merchants of
Hong Kong, Douglas Lapraik helped
provide financial support for the junk
Keying that sailed from Hong Kong to
London via New York in 1847.

93

M. Miller
*A Cantonese Dressed for Chinese New Year,
Canton, 1861-64.*

M. Miller
A Shopkeeper and His Family, Canton,
1861-64.

M. Miller
The Grandstand at the Hong Kong Race Course, 1861-64.

At the time this photograph was taken, there were approximately 700 European residents in Hong Kong, for whom the weekly race meets were almost obligatory. The track and the Club dominated European social life in China in the late 19th century. In 1870, the Shanghai Club spent $16,724 on drinks, and $72.00 on its reading room.

JOHN THOMSON
Hong Kong, 1868-72

Of the three great photographers of the China scene, John Thomson was the last to arrive. What Beato and Miller left undone, Thomson set out to photograph. Eventually, he traveled 5,000 miles in the interior of imperial China during a residence that lasted four years. His culminating achievement was a photographic encyclopedia of Chinese landscape, life and culture entitled *Illustrations of China and Its People* (4 Vols.)

96

Woman, South China, 1868-70.

Canton Garden, 1868-72.

John Thomson
A Girl of the Working Class, 1868-72.

Opposite

John Thomson
Ships in Hong Kong Harbor During the Visit of H.R.H. the Duke of Edinburgh to the Colony, October 31, 1869.

British longboats drawn up in review mark the route the Duke will travel. On the right of the Duke's ship is the H.M.S. Tamar, a three-decker ship-of-the-line which converted to a hulk and was used at various times as a hospital ship, prison and storage facility.

John Thomson
Woman of the Working Class,
Canton, 1868-72.

Opposite

John Thomson
A Scene on the China Coast, 1868-72.

John Thomson
Town Scene, 1868-72.

John Thomson
Shop of Wah Loong and Cumwo,
Hong Kong, 1868-72.

John Thomson
*Chinese Hairstyles: No. 15, A Lady of
Swatow, Kwangtung, No. 16-20, Manchu
and Tartar Ladies, 1868-72.*

John Thomson
Chinese Actors, 1868-72.

Although the Chinese had a great
fondness for theatricals, the profession of
actor was considered among the most
debased and disreputable. A severe course
of training went into the apprenticeship
of an actor which usually began when a
boy was either indentured or sold to a troupe.

EMIL RUSFELDT
THE HONG KONG
PHOTOGRAPHIC ROOMS
Hong Kong, 1871-74.

Rusfeldt bought the stock and custom of
W.P. Floyd, who in turn had bought out
Thomson. The result was that both Floyd
and Rusfeldt did considerable business
printing Thomson negatives in addition
to printing their own.

106

Female Musicians, Foochow, Fukien,
1871- 74.

Opposite

Flower Boats, Canton, 1871-74.

Flower boats were alternately tea houses
and floating brothels.

**Emil Rusfeldt, The Hong Kong
Photographic Rooms**
Chinese Drawing Room, 1871-74.

**Emil Rusfeldt, The Hong Kong
Photographic Rooms**
A Garden In Canton, 1871-74.

W. SAUNDERS
Shanghai, 1864-85.

L.F. FISLER
Shanghai, 1865-86.

Both Saunders and Fisler enjoyed a rare longevity for commercial photographers on the China coast. They specialized in views designed to appeal to the foreign visitor.

110

W. Saunders
Musicians, Shanghai, 1864-85.

L.F. Fisler
Chinese Actors, Shanghai, 1870s.

113

W. Saunders
View of the Countryside,
North China, 1864-85.

W. Saunders
Traveling Restaurant, Shanghai,
1864-85.

L.F. Fisler
Woman Weaving, Shanghai, 1870s.

No. 26.--Sale Pears Shanghai.

117

Opposite

Attributed to L.F. Fisler
Street Vendor Selling Pears,
Shanghai, 1870s.

W. Saunders
Wet Weather, Shanghai, 1864-85.

118

343-Chinese Children

Photographer Unknown
Chinese Children, 1900-10.

Opposite

Photographer Unknown
Domestic Life, the Reception Hall of a Gentleman's House, Canton, 1890s.

Overleaf

Photographer Unknown
Chinese Drivers on the Peking-Hankow Railway, 1899-1905.

Photographer Unknown
The Temple of Heaven, Peking, 1911-15.

At the Temple of Heaven, the emperor
gave formal expression to his divine role
twice a year, at winter and summer
solstices. During the imperial visit to
the Temple of Heaven, Europeans were
given formal notice not to look at or
approach the imperial procession.
After the revolution of 1912, weeds grew
up on this most sacrosanct ground
of imperial China.

Yu, Court Photographer
*The Empress Dowager Posed as the Goddess
of Mercy, Kuan-yin, Peking,* 1902-08.

"The Empress Dowager not only loved to
be painted as the Goddess of Mercy, but
she clothed herself in the garments
suitable to that deity . . . (and) then
called young Yu, her court photographer."
I.T. Headlan, *Court Life in China* (1909).

Opposite

123

DONALD MENNIE
Peking-Shanghai, 1899-1941.

Mennie, a successful businessman and
amateur photographer, produced a series
of intensely romantic views of China,
which were published during the years
1914-27. His delicately shaded effects
were enhanced by the use of photogravure.

Opposite

The Nan-k'ou Pass, North of Peking,
1912-19.
Located twenty-five miles from Peking
and two miles from the Great Wall, this
village witnessed the passage of armies in
triumph or in flight for millennia.

Memorial Arches, Peking, 1912-19.

Memorial Arches, Peking, 1912-19.

Opposite

Donald Mennie
The End of the Road, Camels,
Peking, 1912-19

Donald Mennie
The Hour of Rest, Peking, 1912-19.

In the background is the Yung Ting Men,
one of the seven gates of the city wall,
built 1553-64.

E.H. WILSON
Western China, 1907-11.

Wilson, a collector of exotic botanical specimens for the Arnold Arboretum at Harvard and the Royal Botanical Gardens at Kew, made a series of extended tours of the remotest areas of western China. As an amateur, he imparted a sense of wonder and discovery to his work which had been missing from the photographic scene since the departure of Thomson.

128

O-mi-to-fu Stone, Yi-lung Hsien, Szechwan, July 15, 1910.

The idol is covered by hats to keep off the sun and rain.

*View near the Hupei Szechwan Boundary,
from the Szechwan Side, Ta-ning, Hsien,
June 24, 1910.*

The terracing on the mountain rises up
towards the 4,000 foot peaks above.

130

E.H. Wilson
The Harvard Houseboat at Chia-ting Fu,
Western Szechwan, December 13, 1908.

131

E.H. Wilson
Riverine Village at Hsuan-k'un,
Western Szechwan, June 17, 1908.

132

E.H. Wilson
Temple with Bamboo and Mu Trees
(Machilus Bournei), Kuan Hsien,
June 16, 1908.

E.H. Wilson
View of the Ta-tu River at the Town of
Ta-chien-lu, Western Szechwan,
July 30, 1908.

PHOTOGRAPHY IN IMPERIAL CHINA
by Clark Worswick

At the beginning of the 19th century, before the advent of photography, the popular vision of imperial China in Europe was formed primarily by two books. The first had appeared in 1298 and detailed the travels of Marco Polo to Cathay, while the second, the *Travels of Sir John Mandeville* (1499), was, among other things, probably the greatest literary hoax of all time. In the manufacture of his *Travels,* Mandeville had plundered sundry contemporary memoirs with enthusiasm. One of these was the account of a Friar Odoric of Pordeone, who had returned from China in the 14th century after crossing precisely 10,002 bridges and claiming to have seen a magic mountain — snow white on one side and coal black on the other. There was a garden in Cathay that was Circe-like, related Friar Odoric, and there he had counted exactly 4,200 souls imprisoned in the bodies of apes and cats. This sort of fact drawn piecemeal into the *Travels,* became the incontrovertible truth of Mandeville's vision; it was the stuff of dreams, and had colored Europe's impression of China for literally centuries.

On October 8, 1846, there appeared an advertisement in a Hong Kong newspaper that was to portend a fundamental change in this view. The notice, published in the *China Mail* ran, "Daguerreotype and Lithographic Printing Establishment, Wellington Terrace. Coloured or outline views made of Hong Kong or China Scenery... Daguerreotype Room open from 9 A.M. to 3 P.M." This notice, less than one-half inch high, was followed by another one two months later, announcing that **Hugh Mackay**, originally a native of Edinburgh, had taken over the printing and daguerreotype establishments.[1] For two years (1846 and 1847) Mackay's studio was the sole harbinger of a photographic enterprise that in the next two decades (1850-70) would demystify Asia for the European. More important, with the advent of photography in China, it became possible to document and preserve a millennia-old culture destined for radical, irrevocable change.

Before detailing the specifics of photography in China, it is important to sketch both the political and artistic backgrounds against which the photographer had, in the most literal way, to work. Politically,

China was a closed country to all but a few Europeans before 1860. Artistically, the vogue of *chinoiserie* in 18th century Europe had stimulated the first tentative enthusiasm for a more truthful view of China. In the early part of the century, this interest was partially satisfied by the productions of Jesuit artists resident in the Manchu court at Peking. Among these were **Dennis Attiret** (1708-69), and **Giuseppe Castiglione** (1688-1766), an artist/architect who rose to be the principal member of the Ch'ien-lung Emperor's painting bureau. In 1793, **William Alexander** traveled to China as the official artist attached to Lord Macartney's embassy. He was to provide the British public with thousands of drawings to accompany both the official and non-official accounts of the diplomatic mission (which had incidentally failed in its attempt to open China to more favorable trade conditions for England). Alexander's work provided the enlightened with the first closely observed European view of the forbidden city of Peking and of the infinite variety of the Chinese Empire beyond. Upon the overland return of the embassy to Canton, Alexander became the first British artist to detail the intricate Chinese lock and canal system, the imperial highways and the legendary, huge cities heretofore known only from rumor.

In the 19th century, other diplomatic missions and artists came to China but no European was given the same freedom of access to its interior as Alexander and the members of the Macartney embassy. An exception to the casual and transient European visitor was the ubiquitous presence in Macao of **George Chinnery**. No account of the European vision or discovery of China would be complete without mention of Chinnery and his various tangled purposes. Who would have believed that a painter who regularly exhibited at the Royal Academy and was a student of Sir Joshua Reynolds would settle on the China coast? But this is what Chinnery did from 1825 until his death in Macao in 1852.

For most of his life, Chinnery's geographic location in the world was determined by a series of strategic retreats from his wife whom he described as 'the ugliest woman I ever saw in my life.' The first abandonment had occurred in 1802 when the painter fled to India to escape her; years later she caught up with him and in 1825, he fled once again (at the same time abandoning his creditors and debts in Calcutta), this time arriving in Macao. Thereafter, whenever this formidable female threatened to pursue him, Chinnery would beat a hasty retreat to Canton, the final and enviable haven for the henpecked husband. One of the most stringent rules of the China trade decreed that no European females were allowed in Canton by imperial edict.

Professionally, a man of Chinnery's artistic stature was able to change several European misconceptions about China. Whereas earlier it had been pictured as unreal and legendary, in Chinnery's work China was transmuted into the great picturesque. Although this may have been unwitting on the artist's part, it was inevitable given Chinnery's colorful (albeit erratic) lifestyle and the European penchant for romanticism in the early 19th century. To satisfy this taste for a mystically reverent view of nature, China was promoted as a land of endless rustic scenes. This tradition had such immense appeal that it was subsequently adopted by the new medium becoming the stock in trade of two generations of commercial photographers.

Fortuitously, the Opening of China (1840-60) occurred at the same time that photography arrived on the scene. Although sometimes overly romanticized, and often ridden with clichés, photographs nevertheless managed to capture the ultimate reality of imperial China. 750 years earlier, Marco Polo had tried to convey a truthful image of China to a doubting Europe; with the arrival of the camera, there was finally an incontestable vision of the last great hidden empire.

Though it is possible to date the beginnings of photography in China to the time of Mackay's daguerreotype establishment, the earliest known photograph to have survived is a nine-inch square salted

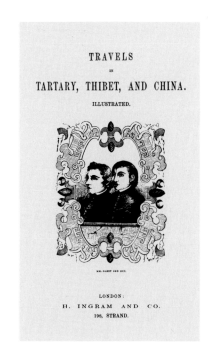

paper print from a calotype negative done sometime between 1850-55 (p. 55).[2] The subject of the picture is *The Five Story Pagoda* (the Chen-hai-lou) in Canton and it is worth speculating on how this photograph came into existence. Only two photographers who were active in the Canton area during this period have come to light. The first, **Eliphalet Brown, Jr.,** was the official photographer for an American expedition led by Commodore Perry which had quartered in the Macao area in August, 1853.[3] However, a more likely candidate for the creator of the print was **Dr. John McCosh**, a surgeon of the presidency of Bengal's Army Medical Establishment. McCosh had taken up photography in the mid-1840s, and was known at the time of the second Burma War (1852) to possess calotype cameras capable of making paper negatives over 20 inches in size.[4] Though it is possible to make only a qualified attribution to McCosh on the level of scarce and delicate equipment, additional attribution can be made on two other levels. Stylistically, the photograph is reminiscent of McCosh's Burma work of 1852, in that it contains a carefully realized central viewpoint. Additionally, in the Indian photographic field, McCosh was the single person technically capable (in the early 1850s) of the difficult manipulations involved in exposing and printing a picture the size and quality of *The Five Story Pagoda*. What remains then is to actually place the photographer in Canton.

An approximate date of McCosh's visit to China can be given as the year 1851. In his book, *Advice to Officers in India*, McCosh offers a certain first-hand knowledge of the difficulties that beset the early photographer working in Canton, before all of China was opened to the West at the conclusion of the Opium Wars in 1860:

> "Canton, this is the last place in the world to resort in search of health. The confinement imposed upon the inhabitants (by the Chinese) is excessive, and one might as well live in a prison. Gentlemen in receipt of some thousands a year are glad to be allowed to rent a pig-stye of a house at the furthest end of a dark and dirty lane . . . strangers dare not, unless at risk of their lives, venture within the walls of Canton, or take a walk in the country without getting pelted with stones . . . they are equally debarred from sailing on the river . . . they are not even permitted to have their wives, or families in Canton . . . there is little or no commerce between the principal Chinese functionaries and the foreign merchants."[5]

Technically, stylistically, even chronologically, it seems probable that this early print was indeed made by McCosh in 1851.

COMMERCIAL PHOTOGRAPHY

Against the background of the last phases of the Opium Wars (1858-60), there appeared two photographers who created the first comprehensive photographic view of China that has survived. More important, these two men, **M. Rossier** and **Felix Beato**, set a standard against which all subsequent photography in China would be judged. But though they played essential, even historic roles in the development of photography on the China coast, they were itinerant practitioners of their trade, who remained in the country for only a brief time.

Rossier arrived in China in 1858, just after an allied Anglo-French force had succeeded in entering Canton, the largest city in southern China. 5,679 members of the Allied Army were hardly enough

to hold the city and, as they wondered what to do with twenty-one million pounds of confiscated tea, the city fell. Rossier photographed the scenes of the conflict with great diligence: a breach in the city wall, a small pagoda occupied by British troops, Treasury Street, a joss house and numerous other city views. In the following year, the firm of **Negretti & Zambra** (which had commissioned Rossier's trip) brought out a photographic first—the only commercially available views of China in a stereographic format.[6] A contemporary review of Rossier's work commented in general and specifically about the pioneer views he had taken around the Canton/Hong Kong/Macao area:

> ". . . We have noticed these views of China at great length for two reasons. In the first place, the vivid manner in which they bring before us scenes so distant, in which every Englishman must feel an interest . . . in the next . . . unless the publishers have a large sale for them, we cannot expect that they will again send out photographers at so great an expense, to such distant regions; and thus, one of the prime uses of photography—the conveyance of information on the subject of people and things we can never see—will cease to be cultivated."[7]

In hindsight, this first review to appear on the subject of commercial photography in China proved to be prescient. It pinpointed the reciprocal difficulties of financing an expensive expedition and obtaining patronage on the China coast. The review was particularly prophetic, since commercial patronage of European photographers was sporadic at best and was to prove the undoing of virtually every European photographer who came to China hoping to earn a living from his work. The review continued:

> ". . . there are a few which possess defects . . . these arise chiefly from over-exposure; but it is easy to comprehend the difficulties under which a photographer would labour in a country like China, and it would be hypercritical to judge them by the same standard which we should apply to pictures taken in England."[8]

Though contemporary British photographic opinion was willing to excuse the technical quality of Rossier's pictures, photographic enterprise in China was advanced decisively the next year by the arrival of Felix Beato in 1860.[9] Beato had come to China as the semi-official photographer of the Anglo-French North China Expeditionary Force which succeeded in capturing and occupying the imperial capital of Peking.

Upon landing in Hong Kong, Beato began to photograph the sights and scenes of the preparation for the conquest. Garnet Wolseley, later Commander-in-Chief of the British Army, described one of the scenes of Beato's first photographs:

> "During the month of March our transports kept arriving daily, disembarking and encamping at Kowloon . . . the ground was quickly cleared and laid out for the troops, wells dug and roads made . . . in a very short time the ground, which previous to our arrival had been but a rocky waste with a few patches of cultivation . . . was covered with tents, horse lines, and batteries of artillery . . . our chief supply of hay was from Bombay."[10]

This description depicts the first large scale settlement of Kowloon (now one of the most densely populated places on earth) and also details the difficulty of supplying necessities to China. The early problems of obtaining adequate quantities of photographic requisites—chemicals, glass plates, spare cameras—were formidable. Added to this was the understandably lethal hostility of the Chinese to members of the expedition. On the march, while accompanying the army, Beato needed to transport large quantities of fresh, relatively pure water not easily obtainable in the height of summer. Additionally, he had the constant worry that his fragile glass plate negatives might be smashed in transit by the dregs of the Hong Kong waterfront who comprised the coolie corps of the expedition. [However, there were compensations. Wolseley, the quartermaster, observed that a single coolie was actually of more general value than any three baggage animals. At least Wolseley didn't have to feed his coolies preciously imported hay, and Beato's anxieties must have been somewhat allayed by his having one and a half coolies to carry his equipment.] From Hong Kong, Beato made a side trip to Canton where he remained during the next few months until the expedition was ready to embark on the trek north. While there, he created large plate photographic views of the city which surprisingly, portray a place of diminished scale and rather nondescript character. Similarly, the imperial highway leading into the city from the north is seen to be merely a worn dirt track meandering to a small gateway of undistinguished architectural interest.

In June and July 1860, contingents of the British and French forces moved towards North China, until eventually a total of 231 warships and transports were assembled off Pei-t'ang. On August 21, the Taku forts, the linchpin of the Chinese defense of the imperial capital, were stormed. Inside the forts that commanded the strategic riverine approaches to Peking, Beato made a series of impressive views that conveyed with harrowing exactitude the cost to the Chinese of defending these bastions (pp. 33-37).

On October 6, the British Cavalry under Brigadier Pattle occupied the precincts of the imperial Summer Palace complex (p. 41). Guarding this was a gaggle of 480 eunuchs who had been abandoned by the emperor when he had fled Peking two weeks before. Inside the Summer Palace complex, the Allies found eighty square miles of park and over two-hundred buildings, thirty of which were imperial palaces. Seen in its entirety, the complex seemed a vast fantasy spun from the imaginations of generations of Chinese emperors. Perhaps more important than the display of imperial magnificence was the cache of imperial correspondence relating to negotiations with the European powers in China. Wolseley, always a trenchant observer, remarked, "Having no regard whatever for truth, bound by no feeling of humanity . . . the cold-blooded rules for government enunciated in 'The Prince' appear to be well understood in China."[11] The shock of the contents of the correspondence, the expedience with which the Hsien-feng Emperor dealt with treaties, and the death of a group of Englishmen and Fenchmen seized under truce caused Lord Elgin, the paramount British representative in China, to order the burning of the Summer Palace complex.

On October 18, 1860, it was put to the torch and for two days (after almost two weeks of extensive looting by the Allies), the palace complex burned, as smoke from the conflagration hung over Peking like a thick black shroud of disgrace. Before this wholesale destruction occurred, Beato managed to take the first (and only) photographs ever made inside the Summer Palace. Though these images are unique as historic documents, they were also a permanent reminder to the imperial family of its feebleness in defending its patrimony. This incident left an emotional scar from which the Ch'ing dynasty would not recover.

On October 24, a meeting was finally arranged between the brother of the Hsien-feng Emperor, Prince Kung, and Lord Elgin who was to accept the terms of Chinese surrender. The treaty was signed and, according to the official British interpreter, Swinhoe, "An attempt to photograph the scene on the part of Signor Beato, was a signal failure."[12] There were happier results on November 4 when Swinhoe reported that

138

Pavillion in the Summer Palace, Peking. From a photograph by Beato.

Beato made his first successful photograph of Prince Kung (p. 40). "Cordiality now existed between Lord Elgin and Prince Kung, the visits were frequently exchanged, the Prince threw off the nervous restraint and show of bad humor that marked the first interview. He sat with pleasure for his photograph before the camera of Signor Beato, and, we are thus enabled to give a view of his far from comely visage to our reader. He is said to bear a strong resemblance to the Emperor."[13]

For the remainder of the year 1860, the Expeditionary Force gradually withdrew from China, having accomplished its primary goal of opening the whole of China to the West. It is to Beato's credit that throughout the military expedition, he managed to create the first major body of photographic work done in North China and in Peking. While in the imperial capital, Beato photographed a series of striking multi-plate panoramas of the city and its surrounding walls. Additionally, he created several single plate views of the temples and tombs that dotted the countryside around Peking. On a technical level, Beato's work is among the best realized in the 19th century, coupling a skillful mastery of the medium with a consistently documentary eye. His arrival on the China scene signalled the beginning of a twenty-year period (1860-80) when the professional photographer chronicled imperial China with a thoroughness that is difficult to believe today. This comprehensive creation of a series of commercially available views is more impressive when seen in the context of all the attendant problems facing the photographer, not least of which was the Chinese belief that the camera was an "evil eye."

At the penultimate moment in imperial China, the photographer's overriding concern was how to obtain patronage. Heat, bad water, inadequate roads, debilitating fevers with no Western medical assistance available — these were the usual conditions under which the photographer labored. But the true miracle of his endeavour was his ability to work while in a state of commercial collapse and imminent bankruptcy.

One consequence of this chronic dilemma was the emergence of *The Firm*. Stated simply, *The Firm* was not an actual commercial entity but rather a huge collection of negatives left behind by all the photographers who had ever arrived in Hong Kong, set up shop, and then gone bankrupt. In time, *The Firm* would come to include the stockpiles of eleven photographic establishments that attempted to do business in Hong Kong from 1860 to 1877. As succeeding photographers went out of business, their stock would be assumed by the next professional photographer who believed that he alone knew the secret of establishing a solid clientele in South China. The memory of each failure must have been particularly short in Hong Kong. Nevertheless, by some quirk of fate, or perhaps because of the professional standards set by Rossier and Beato, the quality of imagery produced by the aggregate parts of *The Firm* remained unexcelled in 19th century Asia. Probably nowhere else during the last century, did so many individuals contribute their talents to a view of one place and period.

The Firm began in 1860 when two peripatetic photographers, **Weed** and **Howard** became partners. Though no first names are available at the 1860 date, it is probable that the former was Charles Weed who later became one of the first and most notable of the California landscape photographers,[14] while the latter possibly became the first partner of Samuel Bourne in Simla (India) during the period 1864-68.[15] Though the suggestion of Weed and Howard's identities is not conclusive at the 1860 date, the possibility that they were men who would soon be founders of landscape photography in places as widely disparate as California and the Himalayas opens the door to interesting speculations about the early development of a truly international photographic vision.

CHINESE SOLDIER.

139

In 1862, the following notice appeared in the *China Directory:*

"Jan 1st, 1861 . . . Mr. **M. Miller**, late operator and successor to Messrs. Weed & Howard, begs to inform residents and visitors of Hong Kong, that he has fitted up the room lately occupied by Mr. Howard, on the Parade Ground, and is now prepared to take photographic pictures of all kinds. Likenesses from miniature to life size, views of houses executed at short notice . . . as his stay at the above place is limited, those wishing his service will please call early . . . a collection of views of various places for sale."

Miller obviously intended to stay for only a short while, but surprisingly, business proved so good that he remained in Hong Kong until 1864. It was during this period (1861-64) that Miller obtained copy negatives of Felix Beato's Peking views and added this work to his own stock of commercially produced images. As a master of the multi-plate panorama, Beato had undoubtedly taught Miller the technique of making these difficult composite photographs. The latter learned his lesson well enough to create his own series of panoramic views of Hong Kong/Macao/Canton which are often indistinguishable from Beato's. Only by Miller's occasional signature, and the fact that Beato used a slightly larger camera can any difference be discerned in the work of the two men.[16]

During the time that Miller was active in Hong Kong and Canton, his great and unequalled forte was the studio portraiture of official and non-official Chinese personalities. Miller's eye was tasteful and incisive and his photographs of the highest classes of government officers and mandarins in Caton form a primary source document of official types in imperial China. Beyond the level of beautifully realized portraits, these images and the series which they comprise, are the most important official photographs taken in China during the 19th century. Despite the limitations of mutual Sino-European bigotry, primitive equipment and slow photographic emulsions, Miller's studio portraits convey a feeling that is almost modern and photo-journalistic.

In 1864, Miller sold his stock of negatives and his business in Hong Kong to **S.W. Halsey**, whereupon he promptly disappeared from the China scene. Over the next thirteen years, a succession of photographers arrived and departed, each of them owning The Firm for a brief period of time. The list includes: **J.A. de Silveira** (1866-67), **William Pryor Floyd** (1868-72), **Emil Rusfeldt** (1872-74), and **Henry Everett** (1874-77), each of whom rechristened *The Firm,* which operated under the respective names of **Silveira & Co., Floyd & Co./** The **Victoria Photographic Gallery** (1869-72), **The Hong Kong Photographic Rooms/The Hong Kong Photographic Company** (1872-77).[17]

While the work of Floyd and Rusfeldt was certainly competent for this period, the only man to rival the genius of Miller in his vision of 19th century China was **John Thomson**, who arrived in Hong Kong in 1868. Like Miller, Thomson was to have a profound sympathy for the Chinese, which together with his great technical mastery of the medium, and his insatiable curiosity about the human condition, he used to artistic advantage. Thomson's association with Asia dated back to his arrival in Ceylon six years earlier; by the time he came to China, he was prepared to make a vast, uncompromising photographic document that would complement the work done by Beato and Miller. Where Beato had created an impressive series of photographs around Peking, and Miller had documented Canton, Thomson would try to photograph the heart of the Middle Kingdom. Whatever had been left undone but was even remotely accessible, Thomson would succeed in photographing during the period 1868-72.

140

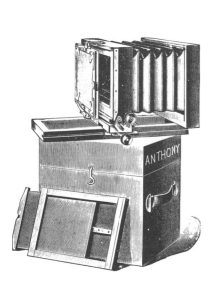

In his first advertisement in the *Daily Press*, on Sept. 28, 1868, Thomson announced that he had for sale: "Views of Hong Kong, J. Thomson, 40 views, 10 large (14 x 19), 26 small (8 x 10), and four of late Dragon Feast." Two months later another more personal notice appeared (*Daily Press*, 11/21/68): "Nov. 21, married 19th, Rose Villa, John Thomson, Esq. to Isabel, daughter of Capt. P. Petrie." Settling down to married life must have been particularly difficult for a man of Thomson's temperament and profession, for when he was not operating his photographic studio in the Commercial Bank Building, Thomson was constantly traveling around China. In time these travels would come to include over 5,000 miles of the inland rivers, the interior and the coast of imperial China.

During his lifetime, Thomson published ten books, six of which concerned China.[18] As a Fellow of the Royal Geographical Society he additionally contributed articles to the Journal of the Society and to the *China Magazine* (the first photographically illustrated periodical published in China).[19] Because he wrote so well and so prolifically about photographing the China scene, Thomson is deservedly the best known of the photographers active at that time. His masterpiece, *Illustrations of China and its People* (4 vol., 1873/4) was the first, best-produced and most lavishly illustrated photographic book ever done on the subject.

No one is better able to describe Thomson's work than the author himself. In 1899, in the second edition of *Through China with a Camera,* Thomson comments on what it was like to be a photographer in the late 1860s on the China coast:

"My impedimenta required for its transport a retinue of from between 8 to 10 bearers, frequently men of evil repute, and dangerous to manage . . . all my negatives were taken with the wet-collodion process, a process most exacting in its chemistry, especially in a land where the science is practically unknown. The plates had to be prepared and developed on the spot, with this advantage — that the negative so taken could be at once scrutinized, finished, and packed for carriage. The practice of such a process in a country where one had to prepare chemicals from raw material implied difficulties to the modern photographer, and in no way was lessened by having to work among a people hostile to foreigners."[20]

In his travels around China, Thomson first went to Taiwan, later moving across the Formosa Straits to Swatow and then up the southeast coast to Amoy and Foochow. From there he moved inland up the River Min to the city of Yen-ing (the modern Nan-p'ing). Jury lists and commercial directories extant in Hong Kong show that Thomson was a resident in the colony from 1868-72, indicating that his travels were not one long, protracted four-year trip as is sometimes implied in his writing, but a series of extended tours originating from Hong Kong.

In 1870-71, Thomson traveled up the Yangtze from Shanghai. At Nanking, he visited the ancient capital where six years prior to his arrival, the Taiping rebellion had finally been crushed and 100,000 rebels had been killed in the defense of the city. From there, Thomson visited the upper Yangtze River and the areas where the provinces of Hupeh and Szechwan meet. On the Yangtze, he kept a loaded pistol at hand to prevent pirates from boarding his junk. The following year Thomson made his last trip, traveling to Chefoo, Tientsin, Peking and finally, the Great Wall.

Thomson departed from Hong Kong in 1872, depositing with W. P. Floyd those views he apparently no longer wanted or needed. After an association with Asia that had lasted for a decade, Thomson finally left China to rejoin his wife in England, where Isabel Thomson had gone earlier to await the birth

John Thomson

John Thomson

相照生介拉安
ENCARNAÇÃO & CO.,

Photographers.

Maloo, House No. 17,
3 doors past

Mr. I. Eames,

Councellor at Law.

of their child. There is an odd postscript to Thomson's departure from China. Ironically, few of the negatives that he took with him were ever printed, except as the original material from which his book illustrations were made. But the negatives he left behind in Hong Kong were printed with relative frequency by both Rusfeldt and Floyd.[21]

In 1877, with the departure of Henry Everett, its final proprietor, *The Firm's* history came to an end and the disposition of all its negatives remains a matter for conjecture.[22] In the preservation and transmission of the work of Beato, Miller and Thomson, the three great European photographers of China, *The Firm* asserts a major claim to our attention. The presence of these three men undoubtedly stimulated higher professional standards in the work of lesser photographers of the time. More important, the three distinctly different visions of Beato, Miller and Thomson have afforded us a complementary and comprehensive view of the life and scene of Manchu China. Because of their undisputed talents, the work of these men might well have survived in any event. It is however in the preservation of the work of lesser known photographers that we are most indebted to *The Firm*. Without it, a large part of this photographic legacy would not have survived.

Co-existent with *The Firm* were other commercial photographers who were active in Hong Kong and South China during the early 1860s. Though none of their work has been known to survive, we can trace the names of **G.E. Petter, C. Parker, Dalmas J. Lagueniere, E.A. Wiebeking** and **W.G. Cearns,** all of whom advertised their photographic services in directories and newspapers of Hong Kong. During the same period, it is possible that a student of George Chinnery, **Marciano Baptista**, was also a photographer of the passing Hong Kong scene. Baptista, chiefly remembered for his fine watercolors, was an occasional artist for the *Illustrated London News*, a scenery painter for theatrical productions and a writer of public documents. His family tradition relates that the artist's photographic specialty and favorite subject was the post-mortem portraiture of Chinese notables at their own funerals.

In Shanghai, 19th century photography was dominated by two men, **W. Saunders** (1864-85) and **L.F. Fisler** (1866-87). Although it seemed initially that the Hong Kong experience might be duplicated in the north with successive photographers setting up shop and then leaving, these two men were able to maintain their commercial establishments and enjoy a relative stability. It is probable that the hand-tinted views of Chinese types around Shanghai which appear in many albums of the 1870s and 1880s were the work of either Saunders or Fisler.

The last of the distinguished European commercial photographers active in 19th century China was **D.K. Griffith**, who worked first as an assistant to Saunders in Shanghai. In 1875, he left Saunders and next appeared in Hong Kong during the 1880s where he managed the firm of **Afong Lai**, an arrangement that affords us an unusual insight into the close cooperation and commercial interchange that seldom existed between Chinese and European photographers.[23] Griffith remained in China for nearly twenty years, spending most of his time in Hong Kong where he became well known as a portrait and landscape photographer. In correspondence with *The Photographic News* (London), Griffith proved to be a sympathetic observer of the China scene (an often rare quality among European residents). Commenting on the difficulties facing the itinerant photographer, he warned, "Travelling in China is at present *dangerous* under any circumstances, but is increased considerably to a worker in our art science . . . I found the natives of Peking not so shy of the camera as the more docile southerners."[24] Griffith then detailed the risks he incurred when he practiced his "art-science" in the imperial capital:

". . . the crowd, having satiated its curiosity, got less pacific, and resorted to the playful pastime of pelting me with stones behind my back . . . jeering calls sounded on all sides of me, until the grand tableau was completed by a huge missile passing my head while in the act of focusing [and] smashing the glass to atoms. I then had to resort to a mild expedient which I have invariably found sufficient to disperse a Chinese crowd. I told the boy to fetch me a glass and a soda-water bottle . . . the crowd intently gazing upon every movement. Leisurely I removed the wire from the neck of the bottle, and with a loud report the cork flew away, and so did the crowd."[25]

Like Thomson, Griffith was sensitive to the cultural differences between the Chinese and the European. He was particularly aware of the special problems besetting the Chinese photographer:

"The native artist has little support from his countrymen, and from this cause none are to be found away from foreign settlements. Some few enterprising Cantonese have tried to push business in a few of the large towns of the interior, but were obliged to withdraw, from the hostility of the natives . . . In my own case I have had my chair torn to pieces on the road, my coolies beaten, and my camera broken . . . *in the case of a China-man he would have fared much worse.* This unfortunate hostility to photographic manipulations is due to a strange belief . . . . that the photographic image is the soul of the original, the withdrawal of which from the body very naturally produces death. This tragic end may not take place for a month or more, but I have heard two years given as the longest time the photographed victim can exist."[26]

It is probable that Chinese photographers had begun working as early as the mid-1840s (possibly as assistants in the Mackay establishment). Throughout the 19th century, Chinese artists working for the export market had copied the productions of European artists,[27] but when photography was introduced, artists in Hong Kong began a lively trade in copying sailors' and tourists' photographs which they rendered into often strangely observed oils or miniatures.[28] While some artists copied photographs, others branched out and became photographers. Throughout the 1860-90 period there was a constant ebb and flow of Chinese photographers. The exception to the rule, however, was Afong Lai, who opened his first photographic studio in Hong Kong in 1859 and successfully outlasted all native and European competition to continue operating well into the 20th century.[29] Though few signed photographs of Afong survive, he was preeminent among Chinese photographers. A man of taste and education, Afong was singled out for tribute by Thomson, who was his contemporary in Hong Kong:

"Retracing our steps to Queen's Road, we pause before a display of huge signboards, each one glowing in bold Roman letters . . . the first we come to is that of Afong, photographer . . . Afong keeps a Portuguese assistant to wait upon Europeans. He himself is a little, plump, good-natured son of Han, a man of cultivated taste, and imbued with a wonderful appreciation of art.

Judging from his portfolios of photographs, he must be an ardent admirer of the beautiful in nature; for some of his pictures, besides being extremely well executed, are remarkable for their artistic choice of position. In this respect he offers the only exception to all the native photographers I have come across during my travels in China. He shows not a single specimen of his work at his doorway."[30]

143

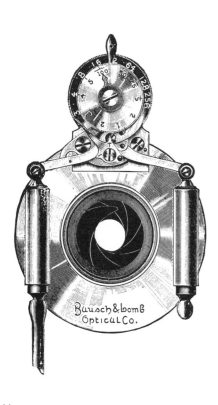

By 1872, there were fourteen Chinese photographers practicing in the colony but in 1884, Baron Stillfried was able to report, "At the present time it is probable that there are several thousand Chinese who make a living by photography."[31] Either growth in this field was amazingly rapid or Stillfried saw competition in every darkened room.

The style and mode of portraiture which the Chinese photographer was forced to adopt was determined by the sitter's perception of classical standards idealized in Chinese painting. In his correspondence with *The Photographic News*, Griffith detailed some of these concerns:

"A direct front face must be taken, so as to show both his ears, and each side of his face of the same proportions; both feet must be arranged so that they are of equal length, perspective being no reasoning power with a China-man. The hands are next arranged so as, if possible, to show each finger distinctly. If they are blessed with a fancy long nail or two, great is their delight to see them well brought out in the portrait. They will certainly have some flowers with them, and a small vase to be placed on a table."[32]

Another insight on this subject was offered by Baron Stillfried who reflected on the peculiar views of the Chinese regarding lighting and perspective:

"In a portrait, the face must be as white as possible; indeed it is usual to place the sitter in direct sunshine. All shading in the face must be removed by retouching, white lead being used for painting on the positive pictures; so that eyes, mouth and nose are merely black dots or strokes . . . . Landscape photography scarcely exists in China, but the Chinese photographer is continually seeking what he can never find — an objective which will produce pictures correctly, according to the native view. He would only be contented with an instrument capable of reproducing the first house and the last house of a street view equally large."[33]

Given these aesthetic considerations it is easy to understand why the Chinese commercial photographer did not relinquish his early training and skill as a painter.

OFFICIAL PHOTOGRAPHY

In the field of government sponsored photography, the camera was used to document public works projects (such as the first railway system), the Boxer Rebellion and the court of the Empress Dowager T'zu-hsi. For nearly fifty years, the Empress had dominated Chinese politics with a ruthless and despotic flair. An understated view of her personality was offered by one of her contemporaries, the Princess Te-ling: "It was characteristic of Her Majesty to experience a keen sense of enjoyment at the trouble of other people."[34]

Despite T'zu-hsi's notorious reputation (she had been accused of disposing of at least two emperors), or perhaps in order to dispel it, she insisted on being pictured as Kuan-yin, the fabled Goddess of Mercy. Her court photographer, **Yu**, was obliged to carry out her request and thus had to orchestrate one of the strangest official photographs ever taken at a royal court. In it, the Empress as Goddess is guarded by Li Lien-ying, chief of the palace eunuchs, costumed and posed as the Goddess' Protector (p. 123).[35] Notwithstanding the eccentric whims of his most famous subject, Yu was both technically adept and aesthetically oriented so that his portraits of the imperial family and their lifestyle remain among the most arresting photographs of 19th century China.

Standing in stark contrast to the amusements of imperial life are the photographs of the Boxer Rebellion in 1900. Possibly this century's first media event, the rebellion attracted a host of photographers from all over the world who joined the eight-nation relief force assembled at Tientsin. Although most of their work rarely rose about the level of topical interest, one exception was the Japanese photographer, **S. Yamamoto**, who with methodical persistence, posed both the besieged and the relief forces in a series of striking portrait groups after the siege had ended. The resulting photographs form a somewhat bizarre museum of military types and martial costume at a rare moment of international cooperation. Inside the besieged legations in Peking, **C.A. Killie** made a documentary record of the life and conditions of the diplomatic enclave under attack. After the relief of Peking, Killie published a series of over seventy copyrighted views of his photographs which are seldom used as historical illustrations of the episode because they are little known.

AMATEUR PHOTOGRAPHY

Considering the great number of photographs taken in China between 1846-1912, it is surprising that so few resident amateurs or visitors created work of lasting merit. Although the amateur had ample time, there was no pressing need for him to finish his work in a careful way. As a result, the amateur photograph is often lacklustre, diffuse and poorly realized technically. In contrast to this, the professional photographer who worked in a climate of commercial vigor, had to produce work that was direct and technically proficient. It is therefore mainly in the work of the professional that we find a cogent view of imperial China. Three amateurs who worked in China in the 1900-10 period proved to be exceptions and contributed work of aesthetic and historical interest.

The first of these photographers was **Ernest Henry Wilson**, who initially used his camera as little more than a documentary tool. A collector of exotic specimens for the Royal Botanical Gardens at Kew and for the Arnold Arboretum at Harvard, Wilson had become a photographer by default. It was only at the repeated insistence of Charles S. Sargent, the director of the Arboretum, that Wilson had brought a camera to China in order to record the locations of the plant specimens he collected. From this modest intention grew a body of work that eventually included approximately 1500 pictures of villages, landscapes and ethnographic types. Not since Thomson had any photographer used his camera as such an instrument of discovery. Wilson made several extended journeys into the most inaccessible parts of western China — into those areas of the Szechwan province where China and Tibet met "at the roof of the world." Fortunately, Wilson ignored his sponsor's advice to confine his picture taking to plants, and thus recorded fascinating views of remote people and places. His photographs are remarkable for their natural quality and their sense of wonder and excitement.

Strangely, Wilson had no interest in processing his own work. Consequently, his glass negatives were transported to England for developing and printing, miraculously surviving the rigors of shipment down the Yangtze Gorges. Perhaps Wilson's ability to be so free and unrestrained in his photography was a result of his being half a year away from seeing any results which might have displeased him.

Contemporary with Wilson were two businessmen/amateurs, **John Arnold** and **Donald Mennie** who documented rustic views of China in similar romantic styles. When he first arrived in China (c.1905), John Arnold was an accountant who later rose to be Secretary of the Hong Kong, Canton and Macao Steamboat Company. The firm ran the principal passenger ferries from Hong Kong up the Pearl River to Canton and, in his official capacity, Arnold had free passage on ships sailing all over South China. He used this opportunity to create a series of intensely moody, carefully conceived views of the waterways in the Hong Kong/Macao/ Canton areas. At first, Arnold's photographs were typical salon creations with textured mattes and Japanese floral decorations on their borders. But in *A Handbook to Canton and the West River* (c.1910), his images of clouds, reflections and the sights and scenes of riverine China acquire a documentary quality of special interest, lifting them above the narrow concerns of genre photography.

Donald Mennie appeared in China during the year 1899. First working as an assistant to Mactavish & Lehman & Co., Peking, he later joined A.S. Watson & Co. (chemists, druggists, wine and spirit merchants), eventually becoming managing director of the firm and one of the most powerful entrepreneurs on the China coast from 1920-41. Although Mennie was a highly successful businessman, his passion was photography. Like many of the pictorialists whose romantic style he adopted, Mennie preferred to work in photogravure rather than primary photographic materials such as bromide or platinum prints. Mechanically produced, photogravure imbued a print with a soft, delicately shaded effect which enhanced Mennie's vision of an antique China. His favorite subject, in which he remained unsurpassed, was the imperial glory of China as reflected in its dusty caravans, morning mist, lakes, bridges and antiquated palaces in settings reminiscent of Chinese classical painting.

The Pageant of Peking (1920) was Mennie's crowning achievement. Printed in folio size, bound in blue silk and containing sixty-six Van Dyke photogravures, it captures the faded elegance of the imperial capital as it was before the automobile or electric poles ensnarled its cityscape. In Peking, wooden memorial arches still straddled crowded streets, and the huge walls of the Forbidden City loomed darkly above every other building in the capital.

★ ★ ★

For nearly half a century, the fate of imperial China had been largely controlled by one person, the Empress Dowager, T'zu-hsi. Upon her death in 1908, the three-year old Hsuan t'ung Emperor was installed on the Dragon Throne, and the final moments of the 268-year old Ch'ing dynasty were at hand. On the 12th of February, 1912, the last Ch'ing Emperor announced his abdication, and when he relinquished the Mandate of Heaven, a world and way of life that had thrived in China for countless centuries came to an abrupt end.

From 1846 to 1912, the camera had been the increasingly omnipresent witness to the Opening of China to the West and to the inevitable demise of imperial rule. Three photogtaphers of this period were unquestionably great artists: Miller, Beato and Thomson. But it is in the work of heretofore unknown photographers like Floyd, Rusfeldt, Fisler and Saunders, as well as scores of other European and Chinese photographers, that the true importance of the camera's contribution to history can be measured. For it is in the mass of attributed and unattributed images that the new medium of photography was able to capture and preserve the look of imperial China. It was an important and formidable achievement.

146

John Thomson
Mitan Gorge, Upper Yangtze, 1868-72.

1. This notice appeared in the *China Mail*, December 10, 1846. According to Mackay's obituary (CM, July 25, 1857), the photographer was resident in China 1844-49. He died in Shasta, California on March 18, 1857.

2. With the invention by F. Scott Archer of the wet collodion process (first published in the *Chemist*, March, 1851), both the daguerreotype and Fox Talbot's calotype process were superseded. The typical salted paper prints (positives) from calotype negatives fell out of favor to the point that by 1855 they were considered antique.

3. "I took a house at Macao as an office . . . and for the accommodation of the surveying officer and the artists to bring their work . . . several apparatus of the magnetic telegraph, the daguerrotype and the talbotype were established and put in full operation." *The Diary of Commodore Mathew Perry*, August 31, 1853.

4. "The ability of John McCosh to produce larger photographs probably came just prior to his departure (for the Second Burma War, 1852) . . . throughout (which) . . . he produced prints measuring up to 20.5″ x 21″." Peter Russell-Jones, *The Army in India* (Hutchinson of London, 1968), p. 167. For another reference to the sizes of McCosh's plates: See, Pat Hodgson, *Early War Photographs* (New York Graphic Society, Boston, 1974.)

5. John McCosh, *Advice to Officers in India* (London), p. 256.

6. A reference to Rossier appears in Albert Smith's, *To China and Back* (Hong Kong University Press Reprint, 1974), p. 32: "(August 25, 1958) Paid a visit to Messrs. Negretti and Zambra's photographer, M. Rossier . . . he complained much of the effect of the climate on his chemicals."

7. *The Photographic News* (London, November 18, 1859), p. 125.

8. Ibid., p. 125.

9. Beginning with the Gernsheims, in their *History of Photography*, virtually every book or article on 19th century photography dealing with Beato states that his name was Felice A. Beato. He himself first spelled his name as Beatto (See: *The Chronicle and Directory for China, Japan, etc.*, 1865-66), then Beato during the 1867-84 period. The first name that he consistently used during the twenty year period he was resident in Japan (1865-84) was Felix.

10. Lt. Col. G.J. Wolseley, *Narrative of the War with China in 1860* (Longman, Green, London, 1862), p. 1.

11. Ibid., p. 244.

12. Robert Swinhoe, *Narrative of the North China Campaign* (Smith Elder & Co., London, 1861), p. 348.

13. Ibid., p. 378-79.

14. Charles Weed was evidently in China in 1860. The following notice appeared in the *China Mail*, "Photographs and Ambrotypes, Messrs. Weed & Howard, will depart for Shanghai by 2nd mail steamer of month." (CM, Oct. 3, 1860). On January 26, 1866 *The Daily Press* stated, "Mr. Weed to begin work in the colony as photographer, was here some years ago . . ." Then on March 3, 1866 "Weed Brothers — Photographic establishment, opposite Daily Press Office." (DP). According to *The Chronicle and Directory for China, Japan,* etc. Weed and presumably his brother were resident in Hong Kong from 1866 to 1867. In 1872, *The China Directory* carried a final notice concerning Weed. It ran, "Fisler, L.F. successor to C.L. Weed Photographic artist, Canton Rd."

15. *Thackers Post Directory*, (Calcutta) 1864-68.

16. Beato presumably had his large plate negatives (approximately 250 mm x 300 mm) printed by Hering of Regent Street, the same firm that printed his Indian views. Samuel Bourne mentions Beato and the firm in his letter to the *British Journal of Photography* (p. 345) during 1863. It has always been a puzzle how Beato's smaller copy negatives were printed and distributed. With the emergence of The Firm in Hong Kong, we get the explanation of how early 1860 material kept appearing with great frequency in late 1870s. The photographs of both Miller and Beato appeared to be great favorites with later photographers who successively owned The Firm.

17. References to the dates of these photographers can be found in *The China Directory*, or *The Chronicle & Directory for China, Japan, the Philippines, and the Straits Settlements* during the period 1864-77. Their comings and goings can also be traced in the bankruptcy notices of the *China Mail*, and the *Daily Press* (Hong Kong).

18. An index and chronology of The Firm would include: Weed & Howard (1860), M. Miller (1861-64), Dutton & Michaels (1863), Halsey & Co. (1864-65), Silveira & Co. (1866), W.P. Floyd/The Victoria Photographic Gallery (1867-72), John Thomson (1868-72), Emil Rusfeldt (1871-74), The Hong Kong Photographic Rooms/The Hong Kong Photographic Company (1872-77).

19. These are: *Views on the North River* (1870), *Foochow and the River Min* (1873), *Illustrations of China and Its People* (4 Vol. 1873/74), *The Straits of Malacca, Indo-China and China* (1875), *The Land and the People of China* (1876), *Through China with a Camera* (2 ed. 1898/99). Additionally, Thomson contributed extensive photographs to the *China Magazine* (Hong Kong 1868/70), as well as all the photographs in the book *The Visit of H.R.H. the Duke of Edinburgh to Hong Kong*, 1869, Rev. Wm. Beach (Noronha & Sons, Hong Kong, 1869).

20. *The China Magazine* (1868-70) was the first photographically illustrated periodical in far-Asia; it contained tipped in photographs and occasionally made mention of photographers.

21. Thomson's negatives were apparently acquired by W.P. Floyd who printed them in his Victoria Photographic Gallery albums (currently in the Essex Institute, Salem, Mass.). When Rusfeldt moved into the premises lately occupied by Floyd (the *Daily Press*, July 24, 1872) he presumably got Floyd's stock as well as Floyd's "Thomson's." Judging from an album in the Walter collection, New York, Rusfeldt in the 1873 period had many of The Firm's negatives, which he actively printed. During the late 1860s and early 1870s, Thomson was the only photographer in Hong Kong to sign his name to his work (Miller's signature had been cropped out when copy negatives of his prints were made); it has been the mistaken assumption that not only were most of The Firm negatives taken by Thomson, but also prints (and whole albums) made by Rusfeldt and Floyd. The result of this mistaken attribution has been that eighty percent of the 19th century photography done in China has been attributed to Thomson.

22. It is almost certain that Afong bought the contents of The Firm. On page 127 of *The Living Races of Mankind*, (Hutchinson & Co., London, n.d.) the *Female Musicians of Foochow* which appears in the Walter album, New York, appears with a credit, "Mr. Afong, Hong Kong."

23. *The Daily Press*, November 9, 1880, "Afong, Photographer, D.K. Griffith holds authority to sign, studio Queens Road opposite Hong Kong Hotel." The reference presumably is to a power of attorney, given Griffith by Afong.

24. *The Photographic News* (October 29, 1875), p. 524.

25. Ibid., p. 524.

26. Ibid., (May 28, 1875), p. 260.

27. At one point early in the 19th century, this trade was so active that the American painter Gilbert Stuart brought suit in Philadelphia to get an injunction against Chinese copies of his well-known George Washington portraits, which increasingly competed with Stuart's original in the American market. Carl Crossman, *The China Trade* (The Pyne Press, Princeton, 1972), p. 133.

28. John Thomson made copious reference to the production of Chinese photographers in *The Straits of Malacca, Indo-China & China* (1875), and he notes the assembly-line approach to producing export-art by Chinese artisans, pp. 190-91.

29. The firm of Atong was carried on by his son Yuet Chan (died, March 5, 1937), but was still listed in the 1941 *Chronicle & Directory for China, Japan* (etc.). It was therefore, by far, the longest-lived commercial firm in China. Unfortunately, during World War II virtually every photograph in Hong Kong was burned by the Chinese residents during the war-time fuel shortage in order to light cooking fires.

30. John Thomson, *The Straits of Malacca, Indo-China & China* (Harper & Bros., New York, 1875), pp. 188-89.

31. *The Photographic News* (London, Feb. 29, 1884), p. 129.

32. Ibid., (May 28, 1875), p. 260.

33. Ibid., (Feb. 29, 1884), p. 129.

34. Marina Warner, *The Dragon Empress* (Weidenfeld & Nicolson, London, 1972), p. 172.

35. I.T. Headland, *Court Life In China* (Fleming Revell, Co., London, 1909), p. 92. Headland makes reference to Yu taking this photograph, as well as to his position in the court. Li Lien-ying was first a cobbler's apprentice. He was rumored to have castrated himself with a cobbler's knife in order to become a palace eunuch. Later, he rose to be chief eunuch, and reputedly one of the richest men in China. "Extortion and bribery progressed from strength to strength under his administration." (*The Dragon Empress*, p. 168).

INDEX OF COMMERCIAL AND AMATEUR PHOTOGRAPHERS OF CHINA, 1846-1912

Anthony, E. & H.T.
Commercial, 1860s; published 28 Miller stereos of Views of China, New York.

Arnold, John
Amateur, 1900-26, South China.

Baptista, Marciano
Commercial, 1860s-80s, artist-photographer, Hong Kong.

Beato, Felix
Commercial, 1860, Hong Kong, Canton, and the North China Expedition.

Brewer, W.
Commercial, 1884, Hong Kong.

Brown, Eliphalet, Jr.
Official Photographer, Acting Master's Mate, Perry Expedition, South China, 1853.

Burr Photo Co.
Commercial, 1909-23, Shanghai.

Cammidge, H.C.
Commercial, 1870s-80s, Shanghai.

Cearns, W.G.
Commercial, 1866, partner in Wiebeking & Cearns. Hong Kong.

Champion, Paul
Amateur, French visitor to China in 1866.

Chan, Nga
Commercial, 1880s, Hong Kong.

Chan, Ya
Commercial, 1870s, Hong Kong.

Cheong, Hing
Commercial, 1869-72, Hong Kong.

Cheong, Kam
Commercial, 1870s, Hong Kong.

Cheong, Wing
Commercial, 1872-89, Hong Kong.

Cheong, Yee
Commercial, 1870s, Hong Kong.

Cheong, Yuet
Commercial, 1870s, Hong Kong.

Cheung, Mee
Commercial, 1890s-1920s, Hong Kong.

Ching, Nam
Commercial, 1860s-90s, Hong Kong.

Child, Thomas
Amateur, 1871-89 (?); gas engineer in Peking who created a series of 192 *Views of Peking and its Vicinity*.

Clark, C.W.
Commercial, 1903, Hong Kong.

Cleeve, Egerton
Amateur; Midshipman, *H.B.M.S. Audacious*, resident of North China in late 1870s.

Dinmore Bros. & Co.
Commercial, 1864-67, Shanghai.

Dinmore, C.
Commercial, partner in Dinmore Bros.

Dinmore, H.
Commercial, partner in Dinmore Bros.

Dinmore, Walter
Commercial, partner in Dinmore Bros.

Dutton & Michaels
Commercial, 1863, Canton.

Dutton, S.
Commercial, 1864-66, Honam.

Edwards, St. John
Commercial, 1872-90s, Amoy; created series, *Views of Amoy and its District, and Formosa, Chinese and Aboriginals*.

Encarnacao, A. & Co.
Commercial, 1866-69, Shanghai.

Everett, Henry
Commercial, 1874-77, employee/owner (?) of Hong Kong Photographic Co., Hong Kong.

Fisler, L.F.
Commercial, 1866-85; bought out C.L. Weed (1871), successor to J. Newman & Co. (1867), first employed at Dinmore Bros. (1866), Shanghai.

Floyd, William Pryor
Commercial, 1865-74; assistant, Shannon & Co. (Shanghai, 1865), operator, Silveira & Co. (Hong Kong, 1866), owner, W.P. Floyd & Co./The Victoria Photographic Gallery (Hong Kong, 1867-72), Shanghai, Macao, Hong Kong.

Fong, Choi
Commercial, 1877, Hong Kong.

Frith of Reigate
Commercial, 1892, Catalogue of Frith of Reigate lists 10 large views and 100 smaller views of China and Japan by an unattributed photographer, England.

Grenier-Caetani, Baroness
Amateur, 1900s, China.

Griffith, D.K.
Commercial, 1872-80s; assistant, W. Saunders (Shanghai, 1872-75), operator, Afong's Studio (Hong Kong, 1880), proprietor of own firm (1880s), Shanghai, Hong Kong.

Grumel & Chausse
Commercial, 1864, Shanghai.

Halsey, S.W.
Commercial, 1864-65, successor to Miller & Co., Hong Kong.

Hing, Mun
Commercial, 1860s-80s retired from photography and returned to painting (1889), Hong Kong.

Hong Kong Photographic Rooms/The Hong Kong Photographic Co.
Commercial, 1872-77; different variations of same firm which was started in 1872 by Rusfeldt who bought out stock of W.P. Floyd/The Victoria Photographic Gallery (1872) which had already acquired the stock of John Thomson (1868-72).

Howard
Commercial, 1860, partner in Weed & Howard, Hong Kong.

Inoue, S.
Commercial, 1880s, Shanghai.

Jocelyn
Amateur, photographed the signing of the Treaty of Tientsin, July 3, 1858.

Killie, C.A.
Amateur, photographed the interior of the besieged legations, Boxer Rebellion, Peking, 1900.

Lagueniere, Dalmas J.
Commercial, 1862, Hong Kong.

Lai, Afong
Commercial, 1859 (?)-1941; most noted and longest lived firm of 19th century China, continued until 1937 by son Yuet Chan Lai and four years thereafter under the name of Afong, Hong Kong.

Lai, Yuet Chan
Commercial, son of Afong, Hong Kong.

Lewis, F.J.
Amateur, 1890s, resident, Hong Kong.

Lun, Pun
Commercial, 1860s-90s, photographer and ivory painter, Hong Kong.

Mackay, Hugh
Commercial, 1846-48, daguerreotypist and first photographer in China, Hong Kong.

McCosh, Dr. John
Amateur; physician who visited Canton on sick leave from the Bengal Army in late 1851.

Mennie, Donald
Amateur, resident, China, 1899-1941; Managing Director, A.S. Watsons; published *China, North and South, The Pageant of Peking, Grandeur of the Gorges* and others.

Miller, M.
Commercial, 1860-64, Hong Kong.

Morrison, Robert
Amateur, photographed the Treaty of Tientsin, July 3, 1858.

Mumeya, M.
Commercial, 1900s-20 (?), partner in Mumeya & Sano, Hong Kong.

Negretti & Zambra
Commercial, 1850s; commissioned Rossier's trip to China (1857-58), published first commercial views of China and stereo series (1859), London.

Newman, J. & Co.
Commercial, 1864-66, acquired by Dinmore Bros. (1866), Shanghai.

Parker, C.
Commercial, 1862-63, Hong Kong.

Petter, G.E.
Commercial, 1861, Hong Kong.

Plemenik, August
Amateur; musician-photographer who visited China in the 1900s.

Rossier
Commercial; trip to China commissioned by Negretti & Zambra in 1857-58, first commercial views of Canton and Hong Kong published in 1859.

Rusfeldt, Emil (Riisfeldt)
Commercial, 1871-74; operated Hong Kong Photographic Rooms/The Hong Kong Photographic Company, acquired stock of W.P. Floyd/The Victoria Photographic Gallery, Hong Kong.

Sang, Lai
Commercial, 1872-89, Hong Kong.

Sang, Yee
Commercial, 1877, Hong Kong.

Saunders, W.
Commercial, 1864-85 (?), Shanghai.

Shannon, R. & Co.
Commercial, 1864-65, Shanghai.

Shik, Kai
Commercial, 1871, Hong Kong.

Shing, To
Commercial, 1872-89, Hong Kong.

Shing, Yau
Commercial, 1877-89, Hong Kong.

Silveira, Jose Joaquim Alves de
Commercial, 1864-70s; clerk to S.W. Halsey (1864-65), owner of Silveira & Co. (1866), sold out to W.P. Floyd (1867) but remained operator of W.P. Floyd & Co./The Victoria Photographic Gallery (1867-72), Hong Kong.

Sing, Yat
Commercial, 1871-72, Hong Kong.

Schoencke, F.
Commercial, 1862-88; a watchmaker and photographer, he was the longest practicing European professional photographer in 19th century China, Foochow.

Tai, Kung
Commercial, 1880s; specialized in multi-plate panoramas of the city in 8 x 12 plates, Shanghai.

Thomson, John
Commercial, 1868-72, author of six books on China, Instructor of Photography at Royal Geographic Society, proprietor of own studio in Hong Kong.

Victoria Photographic Gallery
Commercial, 1867-71; owned by W.P. Floyd who purchased Thomson's studio in 1871, Hong Kong.

Wa, How
Commercial, 1889, Hong Kong.

Weed Brothers
Commercial, 1866-68, Hong Kong.

Weed, C.L.
Commercial, 1850s-71; partner in Weed & Howard (1860), partner in Weed Brothers (1866), sold stock to Fisler (1871), Hong Kong, Shanghai.

Wiebeking, E.A.
Commercial, 1865-66, partner in Wiebeking & Cearns, Hong Kong.

Wilson, Ernest Henry
Amateur, botanist and collector for The Royal Botanical Gardens at Kew and the Arnold Arboretum of Harvard University, 1907-11, Western China.

Wo, Tun
Commercial, 1871-72, Hong Kong.

Yamamoto, S.
Commercial, photographer active in the relief expedition, Boxer Rebellion, 1900.

Yera, H.
Commercial, 1890s-1915, Hong Kong.

Yu (Court Photographer)
Official Photographer to the Empress Dowager, 1900 (?)-08, Peking.

SOURCES

Algood, Maj. Gen., *The China War, 1860: Letters & Diaries.* London, Longmans, Green, 1901.

Appleton, Wm. W., *A Cycle of Cathan.* New York, Columbia University Press, 1951.

Beeching, Jack, *The Chinese Opium Wars.* London, Hutchinson & Co., 1975.

Bredon, Juliet, *Peking.* Shanghai, Kelley & Walsh, 1920.

Carl, Katherine A., *With the Dowager Empress.* New York, The Century Co., 1905.

Cameron, Nigel, *From Bondage to Liberation: East Asia, 1860-1952.* Hong Kong, The Oxford University Press, 1975.

Chvany, Peter, *E.H. Wilson, Photographer.* Boston. *Arnoldia,* The Arnold Arboretum of Harvard, Vol. 36, No. 5, 1976.

Cohen, Paul, *China and Christianity: The Missionary Movement and The Growth of Chinese Antiforeignism. 1860-1870.* Harvard University Press, 1974. *Between Tradition and Modernity, Wang T'ao and Reform in Late Ch'ing China.* Harvard University Press, 1974.

Collis, Maurice, *Marco Polo.* New York, New Directions, 1960. *Foreign Mud.* London, Faber & Faber, 1964.

Cooper, Elizabeth, *My Lady of the Chinese Courtyard.* New York, Stokes & Co., 1914.

Esherick, Joseph, *Reform and Revolution in China: The 1911 Revolution in Hunan and Hubei.* University of California Press, 1976.

Hummel, Arthur, ed., *Eminent Chinese of the Ch'ing Period.* Washington D.C., 1944.

Hutcheson, Robin, *Chinnery: The Man and the Legend.* Hong Kong, The South China Morning Post, 1975.

Jung-pang, Lo, ed., *K'ang Yu-wei, A Biography and a Symposium.* University of Arizona Press, 1967.

Jung, Tsou, *The Revolutionary Army* (translated by John Lust). The Hague, 1968.

King, Frank H.H. & Clarke, Prescott, *A Research Guide to China Coast Newspapers, 1822-1911.* Cambridge, Mass., Harvard East Asia Monographs, 1965.

Kramer, Paul, *The Last Manchu.* London, Arthur Barker, Ltd., 1967.

Huc, M., *Travels in Tartary, Thibet, and China, During the Years 1844-45-46.* London, National Illustrated Library, n.d.

Huc, M., *A Journey Through the Chinese Empire.* New York, Harper & Brothers, 1855.

Lockwood, Stephen C., *Augustine Heard and Co., 1858-1862.* Cambridge, Mass., Harvard East Asian Monographs, 1971.

Macgowan, John, *Lights and Shadows of Chinese Life.* Shanghai, The North China Daily News & Herald, 1909.

Morgan, Evan, *A Guide to Wenli Styles and Chinese Ideals,* Shanghai, Christian Literature Society for China, 1912.

Oliphant, L., *Narrative of the Earl of Elgin's Mission to China and Japan.* Oxford, Oxford University Reprint, 1970.

Price, Don C., *Russia and the Roots of the Chinese Revolution, 1896-1911.* Harvard University Press, 1974.

Scidmore, E.R., *China, The Long Lived Empire.* New York, The Century Co., 1900.

Smith, Albert, *To China and Back.* Hong Kong, Hong Kong University Press, 1974.

Swinhoe, Robert, *Narrative of the North China Campaign of 1860.* London, Smith, Elder & Co., 1861.

Thompson, Lawrence G., trans., *Ta T'ung Shu: The One World Philosophy of K'ang Yu-wei.* London, 1958.

Wakeman, Frederic, *Strangers at the Gate.* Berkeley, The University of California, 1966. *The Fall of Imperial China.* New York, The Free Press, 1975.

Warner, John, *Hong Kong 100 Years Ago.* Hong Kong, Hong Kong Government Press, n.d.

Warner, Marina, *The Dragon Empress.* London, Weidenfeld & Nicolson, 1972.

Woodcock, George, *The British in the Far East.* New York, Atheneum, 1969.

Wright, Mary C., *The Last Stand of Chinese Conservatism, The T'ung-chih Restoration, 1862-1874.* Stanford University Press, 1957.

PICTURE COLLECTIONS

151

The Royal Asiatic Society, London: 17, 26-31, 46, 50-51, 66, 69, 71, 73-75, 79, 88-95.

The Arnold Arboretum of Harvard University: 22, 53, 128-133.

The Forbes Library, Northampton, Mass.: 77, 106.

The Freer Gallery of Art, Washington, D.C.: 21, 22, 123.

Sue Hess, Andover, Mass.: 70, 78, 80-82, 84-87.

R.P. Kingston, Cambridge, Mass.: 62.

Janet Lehr Gallery, New York: 54, 68, 83, 96-98, 101, 103.

Harry Lunn, Jr., Graphics International, Washington, D.C.: 58, 110, 112-113, 114, 117.

Peabody Museum of Salem, Mass.: 100, 107, 111, 115, 116, 118.

Samuel Wagstaff, New York: 20, 49, 52, 56, 60, 64, 67, 99, 104, 119, 148.

Paul Walter, New York: 33-39, 41-43, 57, 76, 102, 108, 109.

Daniel Wolf Gallery, New York: 18-19.

Private Collections: Frontispiece, 23, 24, 40, 45, 47, 48, 55, 59, 63, 65, 72, 120-122, 124-127.

Marcus Ratliff designed this book with the assistance of Patricia Lee Chu.

Marilyn Penn supervised the copy editing and proofreading assisted by Jenifer Ratliff.

The text was photo-composed in Goudy Old Style by Maxwell Photographics.

Peter Gabriel of Quadri, Inc. supervised the production and manufacturing.

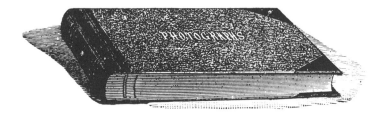